RHYMING HISTORY

The Story of England in Verse

RHYMING HISTORY
The Story of England in Verse

by Colin Wakefield

Illustrations by John Partridge

VOLUME ELEVEN: 1837 – 1858

The Early Victorians

DHP
Double Honours Publications

RHYMING HISTORY
The Story of England in Verse

VOLUME ELEVEN: 1837 – 1858
The Early Victorians

First published in 2020 by Double Honours Publications.

ISBN 978-1-9160537-3-1

Double Honours Publications

Email: info@rhyminghistory.co.uk
Website: www.rhyminghistory.co.uk
Twitter: @Rhyming_History

AUTHOR'S NOTE

This is Volume Eleven of our *Rhyming History* (still in the writing), which will eventually stretch from Julius Caesar's first arrival in Britain in 55BC to the present day.

Volume Twelve (The Later Victorians) will be published in 2021, with subsequent volumes appearing annually. The published volumes are available for sale through our website, Amazon and selected retailers. Volume One (The Romans to the Wars of the Roses) is available as an ebook through Amazon Kindle. There is also a CD of excerpts from Volume One.

These books of verse are intended for those who want to learn more about our history, but in not too solemn a way. I hope they will also appeal to a wider audience, schools, students and historians, and those who simply enjoy reading verse.

Some spellings from original sources have been modernised.

John Partridge has again provided witty and entertaining illustrations to accompany the text, for which I am as ever most grateful.

My special thanks are due to Jonathan Dowie for his detailed preparation of the text and to Janet Marsten for the creation of our new website. I am also most grateful to Alan Coveney for his expert advice on the text and to Pam Weeks for her continuing support.

Please visit our website for updates on future volumes of the *History* and for news of live performances of the verse.

www.rhyminghistory.co.uk

Colin Wakefield – November 2020

QUEEN VICTORIA (1837 – 1901)

Old King William was declining fast.　　　　　**1837**
On June the 20th he breathed his last.
He had given orders, as was his way,
That celebrations for Waterloo Day
(Which fell on the 18th) should go ahead.
Two days later the old codger was dead.

He lived to see the anniversary
Of Britain's finest triumph. This, to me,
Defines his spirit – the epitome
Of patriotism and decency.
The French, I suspect, may well disagree.

When William died, there were real tears.
His brother George's death was marked by fears
Of discontent and instability.
Yet Will, though of modest ability,
Steadied the buffs. The country hunkered down
To a settled future under the Crown.

The background to Victoria's succession

There would of course be regular wobbles
Under the new Queen, family squabbles,
Political storms, but the mind boggles
At the thought of Will's next brother-in-line
Succeeding to the throne. Depraved, malign
And sadistic, the Duke of Cumberland
Nearly made it. Heirs, you should understand,
Were in short supply. George sired one child,
The fair Princess Charlotte, enchanting, mild
And well-favoured. The philandering King
Was father to a veritable string
Of other, illegitimate offspring,

But Charlotte was his only true-born heir.
Then Fate dealt a blow, a sorry affair.
The Princess died in childbirth. Cue: despair.

Her premature death caused a sensation.
Charlotte alone of her generation
Had enjoyed the lawful right to succeed.
Her aunts, sad to say, were too old to breed,
And of her uncles' issue none was fit.
Not one among them was legitimate!

So when Princess Charlotte died, was that it?
Far from it. The race was on for an heir.
Wives were sought any- and everywhere
For the King's dissolute younger brothers,
Viz. the Duke of Clarence, among others,
The future King William. His mistress,
Dottie Jordan, the comedy actress,
Was dumped. The Duke of Kent's was also ditched,
To clear the decks for them both to get hitched.

Kent took to wife a young widowed Princess,
Victoire of Saxe-Coburg, sister, no less,
Of Charlotte's widower, Prince Leopold.
She was all he could find. Victoire, we're told,
Spoke not a word of English. However,
She was smart and shrewd, canny and clever.

Victoria's parentage

Edward, Duke of Kent, was a severe man,
Cruel and harsh (I was never a fan).
He received his military training
In Hanover. There was no restraining
His ardour when it came to discipline.
Savage floggings were the best medicine,

The Early Victorians

In his book, for idle troops. One victim,
A French deserter, threatened (good for him)
To shoot the Duke. This could not be ignored.
Mercy and pity Kent could ill afford.
What was the poor unfortunate's reward?
Well, I can hardly expect you to guess.
Nine hundred and ninety-nine lashes. Yes.
The Duke stood by as these were meted out,
A smirk on his ugly face no doubt.
The soldier survived. He uttered no sound.
He made no complaint as he held his ground,
A case of astonishing bravery
In the face of hideous knavery.

Kent dumped his mistress (I call this obscene)
After twenty-five years, vicious and mean.
His future wife Victoire, at seventeen,
Had been married to a man twice her age,
The Prince of Leiningen. It's hard to gauge,
But the match was unhappy it appears.
The union lasted eleven years,
Before young Victoire was left a widow.
Saddled with a son and daughter in tow,
And short of money, the outlook was bleak.
Her prospects were poor, and worse by the week.

Yet now, in contrast to what might have been,
Victoire was mother to a future Queen –
And she played the part for all she was worth.
But just eight months after her daughter's birth,
Old Kent, her husband, died. Three hundred pounds
Were all her income. The figure astounds.
Without the help of brother Leopold,
The widow would have been out in the cold.

On May the 24th, 1819,
Princess Victoria, the future Queen,

Was born, "as plump as a partridge". What sauce!
She was always a bit of a podge, of course,
But fit as a fiddle and strong as a horse.

The Queen lived to give birth to five daughters
And four strapping sons. The choppy waters
Of Europe engulfed the majority.
These scions of the royal family
(Eight of them, anyway) married spouses
From the diverse imperial houses
Of Waldeck-Pyrmont, Hesse-by-the-Rhine,
Battenburg, Russia, Schleswig-Holstein,
Denmark and Prussia. Out of the nine,
The Princess Royal made the greatest match.
The German Emperor was quite a catch –

The Early Victorians

Frederick the Third. Mother she became
To Kaiser Wilhelm, whose chief claim to fame
Was as Britain's brutal adversary
In the Great War. Victoria, you see,
Was the grandmother of Europe. Mark this:
The good Queen's third-born, Princess Alice,
Was the great-grandmother of Prince Philip,
The Duke of Edinburgh. Philip's kinship
With Princess Elizabeth, later Queen,
Is by virtue of a shared royal gene
Passed down through Victoria's eldest son,
Albert, better known to everyone
As Edward the Seventh. Elizabeth
And Philip are thus – now don't hold your breath –
Third cousins, in a direct line, as they are,
From Victoria, their great-great-grandmama!

I am running ahead. Forgive me please.
Back to the plot, with my apologies.
The wife of the Duke of Coburg, Louise,
Gave birth to a beautiful baby boy,
Albert his name. Just imagine the joy!
A cousin for little Victoria!
One reason for all the euphoria
Was the future design, already hatched,
To have both these infants royally matched.
Victoria and Albert? Sounds good to me.
Would it come to pass? You must wait and see.

Childhood and education

Victoria's first years were far from grand.
The family struggled, you understand.
Apart from the odd visit to Ramsgate,
Mother and daughter were left to their fate,
In a state of relative poverty,
At Kensington Palace. 'Melancholy'

Rhyming History

Was how the Queen would recall her childhood.
Poor and unloved, she was misunderstood,
A martyr to sadness and solitude.

Forgive me now, I don't wish to be rude,
But this we should take with a pinch of salt.
Her temper tantrums were nobody's fault
But her own. Once, out of sheer cussedness,
She threw her scissors at her governess,
Fräulein Lehzen. Yet she called her, no less,
"My precious Lehzen", her very best friend,
Loyal, loving and true. Then to pretend,
As she was apt to do in later life,
That her mother failed her, cut like a knife.
The charge was undeniably unfair.
The Duchess was devoted to her care.

Indeed, the Princess never slept alone
Until the day she ascended the throne.
She shared a room with her mother, it's said –
In fact, I believe that they shared a bed.
There was always someone to hold her hand
As she walked downstairs. Her routine was planned,
To the last detail. Far from being alone,
Victoria's time was rarely her own.

Her schooling was above the average,
By all accounts, for a girl of her age.
She expressed herself "not fond of learning
"As a little child". She was discerning
In her studies. She preferred to be read to,
Rather than to read. This Lehzen had to do.

A tutor was engaged when she was eight,
One of whose tasks was to eradicate
All trace of his pupil's German accent.
Raised as she was by the Duchess of Kent,

This was no mean feat. One would never know
That the Princess was not '*echt englisch*' though –
Apart from the odd, unexpected "Zo!"

The same fellow taught her geography,
Her letters, and some basic history.
Other tutors covered arithmetic
And languages. Though no academic,
These subjects she loved. Dancing she adored,
Painting and drawing. Science she abhorred.
As she grew up she developed a taste
For "the dear opera". Far from straitlaced,
Italian composers she preferred,
Rossini and Bellini. Mark my word,
She relished their wit and lightness of touch,
Although Handel she didn't care for much.

Rhyming History

As educations go, a fair mix:
Languages, science, mathematics,
Geography… But what of politics?
Modern and European history?
The constitution? It's a mystery
How these were overlooked. The future Queen
Knew nothing of the political scene,
At home or abroad. How could this have been?
Was she kept in the dark deliberately,
The victim, poor wretch, of a conspiracy?
This is a distinct possibility.

John Conroy

The Duke of Kent's personal equerry
Had been one John Conroy, a ruthless man,
Scheming and clever. Conroy had a plan.
Private secretary he soon became
To the widowed Duchess. Lacking all shame,
He aimed to be Regent in all but name,
Should Princess Victoria become Queen
Before she attained the age of eighteen.
Conroy achieved a measure of success
In winning over the bereaved Duchess.
The vulnerable widow resented
The coolness of King George (late lamented)
And the less than supportive attitude
Of William, whom she considered rude,
Obstructive and licentious to boot.

Subtlety was never her strongest suit.
She kept her daughter away from the King.
William's illegitimate offspring
(By Dorothy Jordan) were an offence.
Whether or not this was merely pretence
It is hard to say, but it caused a rift.
The Duchess was given pretty short shrift.

The Early Victorians

What also gave rise to some bitterness
Was her refusal to let the Princess
Attend King William's Coronation.
She caused, moreover, great consternation
By sallying forth across the nation
To introduce her daughter, the Princess,
To the people. This caused immense distress
To the King. Indeed, he was furious.
Why did she do this? I am curious.
Conroy's handiwork was behind it all.
To the sly fiend it was the perfect call
To seek to drive a wedge between the King
And the heir apparent. Conroy's plotting
Was luckily of limited effect.
The King was not fooled, as you might expect.
He never blamed Victoria at all.
The Duchess, though, was heading for a fall.

Victoria loathed Conroy. Her mother
Was even rumoured to be his lover.
This was unlikely but, as rumours go,
There was gossip that the old so-and-so
Was Victoria's father. I say no!
Imagine anything quite so absurd.
Stand before a portrait of George the Third:
Take note of the beaky nose of a bird
And the distinctive, hooded, bulbous eyes.
It only takes a moment to surmise
That the Princess has to be legitimate,
The King's granddaughter. It's a perfect fit.
John Conroy, the ass, finally blew it.
He overstepped the mark and he knew it.
Victoria was in recovery
From typhoid fever. Conroy, the bully,
Sought to take advantage of her weakness –
I have to say, this renders me speechless –
By demanding her signature, no less,

Rhyming History

To a vital paper. This document
Purported to secure the appointment
Of Conroy himself, when she became Queen,
As her private secretary. I mean!
Victoria had barely turned sixteen;
She was frail and still in convalescence;
The pressure on the poor girl was intense.
Yet she mustered her courage and saw sense.
She refused to sign. Her mother, she knew
(Which made it far worse), was in on it too.

She never forgot this attempted *coup*.
The instant she was Queen, Conroy was out.
Did she give the benefit of the doubt
To her mother, the Duchess? Sadly, no.
When push came to shove, she too had to go,
A bit-part player, cast in the background,
Victim of the royal merry-go-round.

Uncle Leopold

Victoria was on happier ground
With her Uncle Leopold. He was sound,
Experienced, politically smart,
And held her interests close to his heart.
He disliked Conroy (a promising start),
Who in turn called him "as great a villain
"As ever breathed". One in a million,
Leopold became her principal source –
Barring her beloved Albert, of course –
Of wise counsel and practical advice.

While Conroy skated on very thin ice,
Earning her loathing, contempt and disgust,
Leopold basked in Victoria's trust.
In turn he prepared her, as best he could,
For her momentous future, how she should

(And should not) behave. He advised his niece
On the pitfalls of fancy and caprice.
He stressed the virtue of discretion,
The value of quiet reflection
And regular self-examination.
Though her political education
Was sadly lacking, Leo did his best.

Albert pays a visit

His crowning achievement, Heaven be blessed,
Was the match between his niece and Albert.
The Prince was so good-looking that it hurt.
The royal pair were made for each other.
The son of Leopold's elder brother,
Albert was first cousin (this we have seen)
To the little Princess, soon to be Queen.
The Prince, at the tender age of sixteen,

Rhyming History

With the blessing of Uncle Leopold,
Paid his cousin a visit. She, we're told,
Found him "extremely handsome". This she wrote
In her journal. "His eyes" (I like to quote)
Were "large and blue". We are not to suppose
It was love at first sight, and yet his nose
She accounted "beautiful"; "very sweet"
His mouth; and (to make the picture complete)
His open countenance "most delightful".

I have no desire to be spiteful,
But his elder brother Ernest, though tall,
With "fine dark eyes", would not have done at all.
The Duchess considered him quite a catch.
In fact he'd have made a terrible match.
Ernest grew up like his father, a rake
And a lecher. For Victoria's sake,
Let's thank our lucky stars for Leopold.
Ernest was worthless, Prince Albert pure gold.

"Very bitterly" Victoria cried
When her cousins departed. You decide:
Was she smitten? Well, these were teenage tears –
But love was in the air. Within four years,
Albert of Saxe-Coburg and England's Queen
Were married. Leo could not have foreseen,
Even he, the astonishing success
Of their union, one of great happiness,
A marriage made in Heaven, no less –
Though with its ups and downs, I have to confess.

Pressure on the Princess

I'm ahead of myself again. Conroy,
The scoundrel, had not given up. Oh, boy.
As William grew weaker by the day,
Conroy and the Duchess, as was their way,

The Early Victorians

Sought to convince the innocent Princess
She was unfit to rule – without success.
What a nerve! Having kept her under wraps,
For years, they now ventured to suggest, perhaps,
That she might be prevailed upon to agree
To extend her mother's term of Regency
Until she was twenty-one, three years off.
Conroy was behind the scheme. Now don't scoff,
But he genuinely believed, the fool,
That he and the Duchess were born to rule.

Victoria gave as good as she got.
Leopold, too, when he heard of the plot,
Was very annoyed. The pair even tried
(Would you credit this?) to bring him on side.
Since 1830, Leopold had been
King of the Belgians. A go-between,
Honest Baron Stockmar, he appointed,
Lest Victoria be disappointed
At the lack of time he could now devote
To her concerns. The Baron has my vote.
Conroy abhorred him, called him "double-faced",
But Stockmar was trustworthy and well placed
To offer the Princess timely advice.
He counselled caution, to be precise.

Another incident, hard to ignore,
Was her mother's conduct (the final straw)
Regarding an offer made by the King –
Who sadly by now was slowly dying –
To increase her allowance. On the eve
Of her eighteenth birthday, can you believe,
Her mother wrote back refusing the gift.
Victoria was livid, deeply miffed.

In high dudgeon, the injured Princess
Wrote to the Baron to air her distress.

She would never have given her consent
To the letter. It should not have been sent.
She had never even been made aware
Of the King's offer. How did Conroy dare?
How could her mother presume (she was vexed)
To open her letters? Whatever next?

The new Queen

Within a month King William was dead.
Victoria was sound asleep in bed
When woken by her mother with a kiss
(At six), a token of the tenderness
She felt towards her. I could not care less
For the poisonous rumours. The Duchess
Adored her daughter, the little Princess –
Though Princess no longer. Picture the scene:
Waiting below, to tell her she was Queen,
Was the Archbishop of Canterbury,
The pompous, bewigged William Howley,
And Lord Conynghan, the Lord Chamberlain,
Son of the woman who had lived in sin
With George the Fourth in his declining years.
You couldn't make it up. Both worthy peers
Had pitched up to inform her Majesty
Of the King's passing. "Perfectly happy"
The old soul had been, "quite prepared for death",
As he sighed and uttered his final breath.

The Queen saw them (note the almost hushed tone)
"Only in my dressing-gown, and *alone*" –
Her italics, for this was something new.
From that moment on, her confidence grew.
To Adelaide, the new Queen Dowager,
She wrote the best of letters (good for her)
Insisting that she should stay at Windsor,

For her proper health and convenience,
For as long as she pleased. She showed good sense
From the very start, an intelligence
Well beyond her years, and a confidence
Impressive to all those who witnessed it.

Prime Minister Melbourne

At nine o'clock she received a visit
From the Prime Minister, Viscount Melbourne.
This heralded a glorious new dawn.

Melbourne would stay at Victoria's side
For the next four years, her counsellor, guide,
Her mentor and friend. At their first meeting
She told the Viscount, by way of greeting,
That she desired him and his government
To remain in office, a testament
To her composure, and a clear statement
Of her Whig credentials. No Tory,
The Queen would rouse that party to fury
With her blatant bias. That's a story
For later. Melbourne had brought for the Queen
A speech that he had drafted. Did she mean
To meet her Privy Council, he enquired,
Attended or alone? As if inspired,
She made her first public entrance alone
And read the speech in a clear, bell-like tone.
Victoria amazed her audience
With her spirit, courage and assurance.

The Queen and Melbourne were the perfect match.
She was ill-prepared and starting from scratch,
Little more than a child. Honest and strong,
She could nonetheless have gone badly wrong.
She wrote that few had "more real good will"
Than she. Lacking experience and skill,

Rhyming History

Her resolve "to do what is fit and right"
Was patent. You've heard of love at first sight.
Well, despite an age gap of forty years,
She and the handsome Viscount, it appears,
Developed a passion (platonic)
That many a critic deemed impolitic.
Who cared? Melbourne was a hardened cynic.
His wife had been mad, the alcoholic
And unstable Lady Caroline Lamb.
Their marriage sadly became a sham
When she fell for Lord Byron. She was wild,
She was crazed. They had a disabled child.
Her husband stood by her, cared for their son –
Kindness personified, all said and done.

As recently as 1836
Melbourne himself had got into a fix,
Cited as he was in a divorce case
As an adulterer. Instant disgrace,
You might have imagined. He, after all,
Was PM. He had a long way to fall,
Yet he survived. The case was thrown out.
There was nevertheless some room for doubt.
He and Mrs. Norton, the 'errant' wife,
Were intimate friends, you can bet your life.
The Viscount was lucky, and that's a fact,
To come through unscathed, his career intact.
He was quite unruffled. Was this an act?
Careless he seemed of his reputation.
Prime Minister? Pah! His lofty station
He considered, for his sins, "a damned bore".
Melbourne lacked appetite. Need I say more?

The teenage Queen became his greatest fan.
Her first judgement of him as a "good man,
"Straightforward and honest" never wavered.
It helped that the Viscount was well favoured,

Witty and lacking in affectation,
Malice or guile. There was no flirtation –
Heaven forfend! But she admired good looks.
Melbourne was fit. Once in the Queen's good books,
There he stayed. His fine eyes, dark curly hair
And winning smile drove women to despair.

Victoria's bond with her Prime Minister

Theirs was the closest to a love affair
That there could be between a minister
And his sovereign. Nothing sinister
Should be read into this, you understand,
Nothing compromising or underhand –
Just an extraordinary friendship,
Born of a unique relationship.

At the end of that first amazing day,
Melbourne returned (as soon became his way)
For an hour's relaxed conversation
In private, this the first occasion

Rhyming History

They enjoyed to talk together with ease.
Before long they were meeting, if you please,
Three times a day, a punishing routine
Expected (nay, demanded) by the Queen.
They had regular dinners together,
Went out riding whatever the weather,
Wrote letters by the score and took long walks.
The people were agog. Eyes were on stalks.
But the Viscount took it all in his stride.
The Queen was innocence personified.

What did they find to talk about? Nothing,
It seems, was taboo. It's fascinating,
But their dialogue ranged from the absurd
To the mundane. The Queen, you have my word,
Was entranced, enraptured and entertained.
Their conversation was unrestrained.
Melbourne's wicked but witty view survives
Why Henry the Eighth got rid of his wives:
"Those women," he remarked, "bothered him so!"
William Pitt, should the Queen wish to know,
Was "a thin man, with a red face, who drank
"Amazingly". We've the Viscount to thank
For his thoughts on the Duke of Wellington:
Always pleased to give his opinion
On any subject you'd care to mention
And ever "sensible to attention".

The Queen was learning about history
In a forthright way. It's no mystery
Why she was hooked. She learned that bigotry
And hatred, Protestant or Catholic,
Made her Prime Minister heartily sick.
Both he detested, equally wary
Of Edward the Sixth and 'bloody' Mary.
He told her too about Elizabeth,
How her maids of honour (now hold your breath)

The Early Victorians

Would sleep with the grooms, with a simple screen
To keep them apart. This amused the Queen –
Elizabeth? No, the new one I mean.

Books, plays and opera were much discussed.
Don Giovanni was as dry as dust,
Victoria thought. The PM demurred:
He'd not heard anything quite so absurd,
And made great play of being horrified.
Mozart he adored. He was mortified.
A devoted admirer of Shakespeare,
He rated *Hamlet* as his best. *King Lear*
He liked less. He had always thought the King
"A foolish old man" – this the very thing
That Lear says of himself! He loved Racine,
And recommended his plays to the Queen.
Yet artists he despised: "a waspish set".

The Queen kept a grey parrot as a pet.
Melbourne was smitten. You've heard nothing yet.
They watched her mother's spaniel, Dashy,
Lapping up milk from a saucer of tea.
Was lapping "a pleasant sensation,"
Melbourne wondered? Some conversation!

It seems the Queen's fascination
With her mentor knew no bounds. The word 'gold'
He pronounced as 'goold' and 'Rome', we are told,
As 'Room'. She comments on his appetite:
"He has eaten three chops" (can this be right?)
"And a grouse for breakfast." Trivial stuff,
But the Queen was engrossed, so fair enough.

Melbourne went too far, I have to confess,
On the subject of the awful Duchess,
Victoria's mother. There's no excuse,
In my book, for his level of abuse.

Rhyming History

"Lord M. said" (so the Queen reported it)
"She was a liar and a hypocrite,
"Which" (she goes on to write) "is very true."
Then they both laughed. Now it's only my view,
But as jokes go this was wide of the mark.
The Queen and Melbourne were having a lark.
As thick as thieves, the odd caustic remark
Was one thing. This invective, however,
Was bitchy, cruel and far from clever.
It simply could not go on for ever.

The PM, for sure, got carried away,
Leading his sovereign badly astray.
One further charge we should lay at his door,
More deadly by far. "Why bother the poor?"
He's alleged to have asked. "Leave them alone."
The original words were not his own,
But those of Walter Scott. We've him to thank
For these ugly thoughts. Frankly, they stank.

Melbourne's relaxed style cloaked a heart of stone.
As an arch-hypocrite he stood alone.
History gives him an excellent press.
I beg to differ. For sheer cussedness,
Wilful ignorance and complacency,
Melbourne has no equal. For it was he
Who was serving as Home Secretary
When the dreadful Poor Law Amendment Act
Passed through Parliament, and that's a fact.
Indeed, when the said measure became law –
August the 14th, 1834 –
Melbourne had already succeeded Grey
As PM. It's unthinkable today
That any politician should say,
As he did to the Queen: "You'd better try
"To do no good." Do you want to know why?
"You'll get into no scrapes." How low can you lie?

The Early Victorians

The Poor Law

Social reform bored him. "Very slack,"
Lord Russell thought him. Let me take you back
To the New Poor Law, so-called. Lord Melbourne
Viewed the reform with apathy (nay, scorn),
But nodded through the changes nonetheless.
He had little choice, I have to confess.
The tide was against him. As he voted
(In favour) in the Lords, it was noted
How he swore in an angry undertone.
Yet he wasn't prepared to stand alone.

So he was party to the awful Law.
Poverty was all the fault of the poor –
That was the New Poor Law in a nutshell.
There was no clear incentive to do well
If poor relief was overgenerous.
The dreaded 'workhouse test' was onerous,
Demanding and severe. It spelt, in brief,
An end to the system of 'out-relief'.
It was either the workhouse or nothing.
No charity at home, this was the sting.
To discourage the idle, the greedy
And the indolent, only the needy
And the desperate would be taken in.
Hard labour, confinement and discipline
Would deter all but the most destitute.
The rules were rigorous and absolute.

The Law provided for the segregation
Of married couples, such separation
To ensure the "proper regulation"
Of the workhouses. Make of that what you will.
Another particularly bitter pill
Was the drastic reduction in support
For single mothers. The legislators thought,

Rhyming History

In their wisdom, that illegitimacy
Was encouraged by excess of charity.
They had a duty to promote chastity
By stigmatising the curse of bastardy.
As with the paupers, so with the 'immoral'.
Enforcers of the Law had little quarrel
With the Benthamite argument, that ran thus:
Only the poorest of the poor need worry us;
The more unpleasant the relief, the less the fuss –
In economic terms a definite plus!

The horror stories soon came thick and fast.
The Law was hideous from first to last.
In one workhouse a certain Mrs. Wyse,
A poor inmate, got a nasty surprise.
Her wee daughter, two-and-a-half years old,
Was suffering from chilblains and the cold.
They were given leave to sleep together,
A rarity this. The bitter weather
(It was Christmas) was hard on the poor mite.

When Wyse sought leave to spend a second night
With her invalid child, this was refused.
When she spoke up, she was roundly abused,
Dragged downstairs and locked in the workhouse cage,
Without food or water, I kid you not.
She was given no coat, no chamber pot,
No bedding or straw, alone overnight,
At minus twenty degrees Fahrenheit.
She nearly froze to death. Need I say more?

I could cite other cases by the score.
Charles Dickens caught the mood. His first success,
The Pickwick Papers, is all fun, brightness
And jollity, a beguiling cocktail
Of froth and nostalgia. How could it fail?

The Early Victorians

In *Oliver Twist* he puts the boot in.
Dickens condemns the cruel discipline
Of the workhouse. "Please sir, I want some more!" –
Not the stuff of an entertaining score
For some musical or other nonsense,
But a moving story of conscience,
Exposing the nightmare of the Poor Law
In all its horror, as never before.

Lord Melbourne, far from recommending the book,
Advised against giving it a second look.
"It's all about workhouses," he told the Queen,
"And coffin makers," things better left unseen.
I find these sentiments faintly obscene.

Rhyming History

"I don't like such things. I don't like to see
"Them represented." Now it seems to me
That the Queen was given rotten advice.
Britain was awash with poverty, vice,
Cruelty, crime and destitution.
Wilful blindness was no solution.

If you take the trouble to dig around
In his Lordship's political background,
You will find much to shock you. For starters,
There's the case of the Tolpuddle Martyrs.
Melbourne's tenure as Home Secretary
Was drawing to a close, but it is he
Who must shoulder responsibility
For the famous events of '34.
The emerging Trades Unions, he swore,
Were in conflict with economic law.
They were "inconsistent… and contrary
"To the law of nature". Melbourne, you see,
Was a firm believer in *laissez-faire*.
Fear of disorder drove him to despair.

So when food riots and widespread unrest
Gripped the nation, he rose to the test.
In the run-up to the Great Reform Bill,
Melbourne demonstrated an iron will
In pressing the hesitant magistrates
To enforce the law. As one contemplates
The punishments suffered by young and old,
Poor ignorant rustics, the blood runs cold:
Draconian measures for minor crimes,
Hangings, transportation – violent times.
Rough justice they called it, par for the course.
Farmers and landowners wore themselves hoarse
In praise of our hero's behaviour –
Cool under fire, Melbourne their saviour.

The Early Victorians

The Tolpuddle Martyrs

As the Union Movement grew stronger
And the shadows of unrest grew longer,
The government cast about for new ways
Of bringing it to heel. Melbourne won praise
For dredging up a long-forgotten law,
Relating to mutiny on the Nore
In the dark days when Britain was at war.
Whatever, you may ask, had this to do
With Unions? Nothing directly, true,
But Melbourne, an imaginative chap,
Discovered, for his sins, an overlap.

The aforesaid law made it an offence
To swear secret oaths. It made perfect sense
To apply this to those Societies
Where such oaths were sworn. Melbourne, if you please,
Wrote to the courts, urging them to take note.
"Perhaps you will be able" (here I quote)
"To make an example by such means." Well,
This policy failed to sound the death-knell
Of the Movement, but it was a close call.

At Tolpuddle they weren't prepared at all
For the storm ahead. They took oaths, you see,
As part of a solemn ceremony
To mark their joining the 'Society',
Or 'Union'. So they were arrested!
Had they sworn? They readily confessed it,
But where was the harm? These sons of the soil,
On less than nine bob a week for their toil,
Faced the law in its full severity,
For simply having the temerity
To stand shoulder to shoulder with their peers.
Trades Unions fuelled the darkest fears

Of the Establishment. The men accused
Stood trial at the Assizes, abused
And humiliated, their legs and hands
In manacles. From what one understands,
Melbourne took a personal interest
In the prisoners' fate. This was his test:
Were the workers' characters good or bad?
Word was returned (this is sadder than sad)
That the men were corrupt, wicked and rough.

This, for the Viscount, was more than enough.
When the pitiful souls were found guilty
And given the maximum penalty –
Transportation, alas, for seven years –
Melbourne declined to intervene. No tears

The Early Victorians

Did he shed. The law in its full rigour
Would be enforced with vision and vigour.
These verdicts and this cruel punishment
Roused the entire working class movement
To furious protest. Did Melbourne care?
Not a bit! He was blithely unaware
Of putting a foot wrong. He remained firm.
The working classes had lessons to learn.
Law and order were his only concern.
"The sole duty of government," he said,
"Is to prevent crime" (he took this as read)
"And to preserve contracts." He was on song.
A massive crowd, some thirty thousand strong,
Marched down Whitehall. Melbourne showed no remorse.
He would never be cowed by shows of force.

Child labour

Interference with economic laws
Was one of the more significant flaws
Of the Factory Acts. By '33,
Child labour in the textile industry
Was only lawful from the age of nine.
Eight and under, that's where they drew the line.
Between the ages of nine and thirteen
Children's hours (the employers weren't keen)
Were limited by law to eight a day.
The work was onerous, needless to say,
Dangerous to boot, with low rates of pay.
Aged fourteen and over, hours increased
To twelve a day. There was progress, at least:
Provision was made for one meal break –
Children still had to eat, for pity's sake.

Where did Melbourne stand on this? The spirit
Of the law offended him. To limit
Employers' rights? His heart was not in it.

With some reluctance he sponsored the Bill
In the House of Lords, but soon had his fill.
"Damn it all!" he complained. He did his bit,
But sadly foresaw little of profit.
A social reformer? Come off it.

The young Queen

Well, so much for Melbourne. What of the Queen?
Her PM counselled her (this we have seen)
Not to concern herself with poverty.
The major issues facing the country
Were problems she could surely do without.
She wrote in her journal: "Dawdled about."
As idle and dull as the day is long,
Victoria could have gone badly wrong –
Had it not been for the likes of Stockmar,
Sir Robert Peel (a particular star)
And her one true love, Prince Albert, of course.

Melbourne, though, was a formidable force.
For the first four years of the young Queen's reign
He was there by her side, to take the strain,
To talk, to listen and to entertain.
But for all his skills he was second-rate,
Only rarely punching above his weight.

The Coronation

June the 28th, 1838,   **1838**
Was the day of the Queen's Coronation.
The Archbishop caused some consternation
By attempting to fit Victoria's ring
On the wrong finger! Poor man, he "knew nothing,"
The Queen wrote, with no small measure of pity.
"He ought to have delivered the Orb to me,
"But I had already got it." Quiet clearly,

The Early Victorians

The ceremony had been ill-organised.
'Lord M.' was in charge, so I'm faintly surprised.
The Queen nonetheless took it all in her stride.
Melbourne, the softie, gazed at her dewy-eyed,
As she took her vows. He was fighting back tears.

The Queen was greeted with tumultuous cheers
On her way to the Abbey. From far and wide
The people arrived, many taking a ride
(A singular adventure) on the railway.
Truly it had been a spectacular day,
Blue skies and midsummer heat. 'The Queen's weather'
Would become proverbial. Altogether,
Victoria wrote in her journal that night,
She would ever look back with pride and delight
At the joy expressed at her Coronation.
Proud she was "to be Queen of *such* a *Nation*".

The Flora Hastings affair

The euphoria was not set to last.   **1839**
Trouble was afoot. The Queen was aghast
At the news that a lady-in-waiting
(To the Duchess of Kent) was suffering
From a noticeable 'increase in girth'.
When would Lady Flora Hastings give birth?

This was the subject of gossip and mirth,
To some, though certainly not to the Queen.
Lady Flora was unmarried: obscene,
Insupportable and beyond the pale.
One further factor in this sorry tale
Was Flora's closeness to Sir John Conroy.
Folk put two and two together. Oh, boy!

"We have no doubt," wrote the Queen (she was riled)
"That she is – to use the plain words – with child."

Rhyming History

She consulted Melbourne. What should they do?
Wait and see was his advice (nothing new),
But as the scandal and the rumours grew,
The Queen ordered the royal physician
To offer his considered opinion
On Flora's 'unusual' condition.

Sir James Clark, we're assured, was incompetent,
But was accurate at least to this extent:
He found no evidence of a pregnancy.
Lady Flora was a virgin. It was she,
And she alone, who behaved with dignity,
Courage and a rare measure of fortitude.
The impulsive Queen (I don't wish to be rude)
Was hasty, ungenerous, hostile and crude.

Poor Lady Flora had a deadly tumour
(Undiagnosed) – hardly the stuff of rumour.
How Sir James could have missed it, I'm curious.
Lord Hastings, Flora's brother, was furious
At the way his kid sister had been treated.
The affair became increasingly heated.
He wrote to the PM demanding redress.
Fearful of further rancour and bitterness,
Melbourne wrote back declaring the matter closed.
This fanned the flames. Nobody could have supposed
That Hastings would be satisfied. In a rage
He published the letters. They made the front page.

The rumours were never traced to the Queen,
Not directly, but this child of nineteen,
Moral to a fault, intrusive and mean,
Was forever closely identified
With the tragedy. Before Flora died,
She visited the poor woman's bedside –
A politic move, it can't be denied,

But too little, too late. Oh, how she cried!
"Poor Lady Flora!" Melbourne, mortified,
Foresaw the danger and was horrified.

The Queen's popularity took a nose-dive,
As her enemies went into overdrive.
She was loudly hissed, driving at Ascot,
By a brace of Tory ladies! Great Scott!

Political difficulties

This was not all. The government was weak.
The future outlook for Melbourne was bleak.
The Whigs' Commons majority was slim,
With the PM dependent on the whim
Of his colleagues as well as the Tories.
That greatest of legislative glories,

Rhyming History

The Reform Act, was all but forgotten.
There was something decidedly rotten
In the state of the nation: recession,
Riots, hunger, economic depression,
With no likely prospect of improvement.

The birth of a new working-class movement,
Chartism, caused no small measure of panic.
The current system was 'undemocratic',
That was the grouse of the Chartists. Six reforms
They sought, challenging the political norms
As they then stood: a vote for every man
Aged twenty-one and over; an outright ban
On the property qualification
For MPs; proper remuneration
For Members; a secret ballot to protect
Electors; boundaries defined to respect
Numbers of voters *per* constituency;
And annual elections (finally)
To Parliament. It's a total disgrace
That this list, now accepted as commonplace
(The sixth apart), should have caused such a rumpus.

It was a clear case, of course, of 'them' and 'us'.
For universal suffrage (albeit male),
And similar outrages, were doomed to fail.
Dump the property qualification?
Let in the riff-raff? An aberration!
Whigs and Tories alike were duly appalled.
'Democracy', or whatever it was called,
Was a recipe for revolution.
The People's Charter was no solution –
The cause, rather, of political unrest.
Future governments would be put to the test,
But Melbourne resolved to do his level best
To ignore the challenge. He was good at that.
The PM was not so much a diplomat

As a coward. One organisation,
The Anti-Corn Law Association,
He refused point blank to recognise at all.
Britain's Corn Laws had 'Prime Minister's Downfall'
Written all over them. We'll pass quickly on.
Viscount Melbourne and the Whigs were long gone
By the time the courageous Robert Peel
Split the Tories over Corn Law repeal.
That's a story for later. Melbourne, for now,
Faced crises on every front, and how.

Melbourne resigns

Ireland… religion… many a headache
Melbourne suffered, exploiting the give and take
Of party politics to cling to office.
It was Jamaica, though, a poisoned chalice,
That triggered the PM's resignation.
Trouble caused by the emancipation
Of Jamaican slaves appalled the nation.
Rebellion and the risk of anarchy,
Exacerbated by the planters, sadly,
Led the government in London to suspend
The Jamaican constitution. The end?
Well, if not to the strife in the West Indies,
Then surely of Melbourne. He was on his knees.
The House of Commons vote gave the government
A majority of five. Ever the gent,
He knew that he could go on no longer.

The Tories were daily growing stronger.
Sir Robert Peel was waiting in the wings.
For Melbourne, well, it was one of those things.
He spurned the rewards that high office brings.
In a tearful audience with the Queen,
The PM resigned. It was quite a scene.

Rhyming History

Victoria was distraught. Melbourne's eyes
Brimmed with tears, the most poignant of goodbyes.
"You will not forsake me?" she cried at last.
"Never," he assured her. She was aghast,
Overwhelmed, at the horrible prospect
Of losing her friend, her happiness wrecked.

Enter Sir Robert Peel

Melbourne advised her, as he knew he must,
To send for Wellington. As dry as dust,
The Duke had the sense to rule himself out –
Too old by half, he had simply no doubt,
And deaf to boot. The Queen should send for Peel.
Sir Robert was her man. How did she feel?
"In a state of agony and despair" –
Poor soul! For Sir Robert lacked Melbourne's flair,
His natural warmth, his honest good cheer.
The Queen knew her own mind. She made it clear
That she refused to dissolve Parliament,
That Wellington should join the government,
And that she and the outgoing PM
Would meet whenever they wished. To condemn
The Queen for forcing these terms is tempting.
Peel's response was nonetheless breathtaking.

The bedchamber crisis

He consented readily to all three!
He foresaw no present difficulty
In humouring Victoria. That said,
The young Queen received with a sense of dread
(And smouldering fury) Peel's insistence,
Sought as a simple mark of confidence,
That she should make changes to her household.
These were neither particularly bold

The Early Victorians

Nor radical. A few ladies, no more,
Were all he asked. There was trouble in store.
The Queen's household, as it currently stood,
Was predominantly Whig. The Queen should,
Peel felt, appoint a few Tories instead –
A modest request, but the Queen saw red.
She would keep her ladies, every one.
She was Queen of England, all said and done.
She would do just as she pleased. Peel demurred.
A complete change would be clearly absurd,
But the poor man was not pushing for that.
The Queen wrote to Melbourne. I'll eat my hat
If she was honest in what she told him.
Peel was insisting, she claimed, on a whim,
On the dismissal of all twenty-five
Of her bedchamber ladies. Saints alive!
Melbourne, supported by his Cabinet,
Urged her royal Majesty not to fret.
They stood by her to a man! As for Peel,
He could not believe it. Was this for real?

Melbourne should never have proffered advice.
Unhappy at having to sacrifice
His privileged place in the royal set,
His favoured life as Victoria's pet,
He was demonstrably unqualified
To give unbiased counsel. The Queen cried
When she lost him, but how she glorified
In Peel's come-uppance. He refused to serve.
She re-appointed Melbourne. What a nerve!

Exit Peel

Strange to say, she later became a fan.
For now she wrote: "I never saw a man
"So frightened." Victoria then let slip
That poor Peel had made the premiership

Dependent on the removal of some,
Not all, of her ladies. Melbourne, her chum,
Was mortified, but nonetheless content
To serve in his place. Was it time well spent?
Sadly not. Melbourne managed two more years.
The Queen quickly rallied and dried her tears,
As wilful and as selfish as ever.
Little by way of spirit, endeavour
Or reform distinguished this government.
Torpor and drift were as far as it went.

Marriage plans

Queen Victoria was twenty years old.
The subject of matrimony, we're told,
Was odious to her. King Leopold,
Her trusted counsellor, uncle and friend,
Had other ideas. It's vain to pretend
That the Queen was unaware of his plan.
Prince Albert of Saxe-Coburg was the man,
Victoria's cousin. The young Princess
Had felt nothing but joy and happiness
When she first met Albert in '36 –
"So sensible, so kind" (the perfect mix)
"And so good and so amiable too."
Though her cousin had been too young to woo,
It was widely assumed by one and all
That this was a love match. Albert was tall,
Extremely good-looking and, at sixteen,
The most beautiful youth she had ever seen.

It was over three years since they had met.
The two were made for each other and yet,
Strange to say, there was no sense of hurry.
The Queen had time on her side. Why worry?
She was savouring her independence,
Her royal authority. It made sense,

The Early Victorians

To her (and this was surely no disgrace),
To balk at having to take second place
To a husband. This was unfair, one feels,
On poor young Albert, left kicking his heels.

Leopold was grooming him for the role.
Albert was amenable, on the whole,
To his uncle's efforts. Yet it was tough.
Was a vague expectation enough?
Was the Queen serious? Not many knew,
Though Melbourne, of course, was one of the few.

He urged her to marry… but Albert? No.
The Prince was a pleasant enough fellow,
But Germans had never been popular.
Careful to keep his comments jocular –
The Queen herself was a Coburg, of course –
He feared a foreigner from any source
(Russia, even) would be unwelcome.
Melbourne was also less happy than some
At the idea of a royal match
Between first cousins. There was just one catch.
If foreigners were out, and cousins too,
Who was left in the frame? Nobody knew.
It would certainly cause a fair to-do
To marry a subject. Better to wait,
Melbourne advised, rather than set a date.

While the PM was busy tarrying,
Albert's mind was focused on marrying.
Victoria was nervous. Melbourne's views,
Sound and well-argued, were comforting news.
The Queen wrote to good Uncle Leopold –
In terms that sounded increasingly cold –
To stress that she had made no firm promise
Of marriage. All she would say was this:
Any prospect of future wedded bliss

Rhyming History

With Albert (whom she referred to by name)
Was two or three years distant. If he came,
On a visit, he should be made aware
Of her clear resolve (this was only fair)
Not to marry. She had "great repugnance"
To the whole notion. Her reluctance
Hardly troubled her uncle. But Albert?
It is fair to say he was rather hurt.

The Queen of England was no great beauty,
Folk were agreed. Albert's sense of duty
Trumped any doubts he harboured on that score.
The Queen was stubborn, a bit of a bore,
And prone to sudden outbursts of temper.
Albert was soft and gentle, remember.
How would he cope? Was it worth the candle?
Victoria R. – too hot to handle?

King Leopold, as usual, took charge.
He was far from downhearted, by and large.
Once the pair had renewed their acquaintance,
Weighed each other up, enjoyed the odd dance
And relaxed in the other's company,
All he foresaw was joy and harmony.

A proposal

Uncle, of course, was absolutely right.
The couple met. It was love at first sight –
On Victoria's part, at least. Three years?
Forget it! Within a trice there were tears,
But of rapture, felicity and bliss.
Her happiness, impossible to miss,
Was instant. She caught Albert unawares.
She was standing at the top of the stairs
When he and his brother Ernest arrived.
"I beheld Albert" (her words have survived)

The Early Victorians

"Who is *beautiful*." His "exquisite nose",
His mouth, "with delicate moustachios",
Were very much to Victoria's taste,
Along with his broad shoulders and "fine waist".

Victoria was the one to propose.
The Queen herself, as everyone knows,
Was forced to take the initiative.
To propose to a Queen? This, as I live,
Was counter to all royal *etiquette*.

Hers was a choice she would never regret.
The Prince was a "perfect being," she wrote,
"An angel". It's worth pausing to take note
That her "beloved Albert", sad to say,
Was far from being flavour of the day.
The criticism, as far as it went,
Was directed at the Duchess of Kent,
Victoria's unscrupulous mother,
And Leopold, the Duchess's brother,
For favouring Germans at the expense
Of the British. It was complete nonsense,
In effect, to deny a Coburg *coup*.
A penniless Prince simply would not do.

Yet Victoria's 'English' family
Protested in vain. Their hostility
Manifested itself in downright spite.
Tories in Parliament took delight
In voting a mere thirty thousand pounds
To Albert, not as handsome as it sounds,
Given that they settled some fifty grand
On Leopold when he took Charlotte's hand,
Heiress apparent to the throne. The Queen
Was furious. Nor could she have foreseen
That her desire to name him Prince Consort
Would be thwarted outright. She was distraught.

Rhyming History

It took seventeen years before Albert
Was created Consort, his just desert.

Marriage

It was a cold, bleak February day   **1840**
For the royal wedding. Crowds lined the way,
Supportive and jubilant, come what may.
The Duke of Sussex gave his niece away
In St. James's Palace, the Chapel Royal.
To the Whigs, as ever, the Queen was loyal:
The congregation of three hundred
Included just six Tories. She blundered,
But the guest list came as no great surprise.
She would have "only those who sympathise" –
Wholly predictable, but hardly wise.

For this was "*my* marriage". Heavens above!
What of the bridegroom? When push came to shove,
Was he a cipher? The Queen was in love,
No doubt at all about that. As a wife,
This was "the happiest day of my life".
She describes her wedding night. They undressed.
Her adored Albert, her "dearest, dearest",
Of such "beauty, sweetness and gentleness",
Spoke in terms of the deepest tenderness,
The like of which she had never heard before.

Then "we both went to bed" (this bit I adore) –
"Of *course* in *one* bed, to lie by his side
"On his dear bosom". True love? You decide.
The Queen was head over heels, that's for sure.
Her love was genuine, constant and pure.
Prince Albert himself is harder to read.
The catty Duchess of Bedford, indeed,
Doubted his passion. His German reserve
She mistook for indifference. What a nerve.

The following morning the Queen found time
To write to her uncle. This is sublime:
She was "the happiest, happiest being
"That ever existed". She wrote with feeling:
"To look into those dear eyes is enough
"To make me adore him." Wonderful stuff.

Early difficulties

Yet the early days of their married life
Were far from easy. Both husband and wife
Had fixed expectations. This gave rise
To almighty rows. It is no surprise,
Given Albert's character, and the Queen's,
That domestic tensions behind the scenes
Ran deep. At risk of sounding dramatic,
Victoria's temper was volcanic,

Rhyming History

Her furious outbursts legendary.
Albert, far from being sedentary,
Preferred to turn and walk the other way.
He deserved better. Good for him, I say.

So, what was the problem? The Queen made plain,
In terms, that politics were to remain
Solely and exclusively her domain.
Albert, possibly, to help take the strain,
Could stand by her side and pass the blotter!
Why should he not be content to potter,
Walk the dogs, command the servants perhaps,
And go out hunting with some of the chaps?
This was far from being the Prince's plan –
Or Leopold's, come to that. A good man,
He wished to lead a useful, active life.
He was young and strong. It cut like a knife
To be classed as a servant, a mere boy,
The Queen's minion, Victoria's toy.

Albert was not even allowed a voice
In choosing a secretary. His choice
Was vetoed. Melbourne's ex-secretary,
George Anson, served in that capacity.
Albert reluctantly gave his consent,
While making clear his profound discontent.
He and Anson rubbed along pretty well,
As it happened. As far as one can tell,
Albert was an accommodating man,
Open and honest. You'll find I'm a fan.

Better relations

From passing the Queen's blotter, it appears,
Within the fleeting passage of two years
The atmosphere was totally transformed.
Victoria's character had reformed.

The Early Victorians

She 'dwindled' into a submissive wife –
Passionate still, you can bet your life –
While Albert, 'the blotter', assumed the role
Of her secretary. This, on the whole,
Meant he moved from handing the Queen her speeches
To drafting them. Into the furthest reaches
Of political life the Prince extended
His influence. As Leopold intended,
Albert soon ruled the roost. This we shall see.

Albert's growing authority

It started with the Queen's first pregnancy.
Taking on the role of secretary,
He quickly found he had far more to do.
Where formerly his duties had been few,
His influence increased, as if by stealth.
The Queen, with child, had to look to her health.
As Albert gained domestic authority,
So he assumed a new seniority
In matters political. It was slow,
This process, but crucial. You should know
That it was decreed by Parliament
(Ever cautious) that in the event
Of Victoria's death in childbirth, he,
Prince Albert, would assume the Regency.
This was a vote of confidence indeed.
In September of the same year, we read,
He was sworn in to the Privy Council.
The powers-that-be had sugared the pill.

The Prince's accomplishments

Albert, in short, was a breath of fresh air.
He was cultured (in a Prince this is rare),
A fellow of commanding intellect,
A fine musician and architect.

Rhyming History

His interests embraced technology,
Politics, science and philosophy.
Albert's *Lieder* (prepare to be impressed)
Bear comparison with the very best.
A gifted composer and organist,
He had rougher arts to add to the list.
A farmer and agriculturalist,
He turned sewage into fertiliser.

He designed for the Queen, to surprise her,
Exquisite items of jewellery.
At Windsor he established a dairy,
Still in use today. On the Isle of Wight
He rebuilt, to Victoria's delight,
Osborne House. Intricate beyond measure,
This unique architectural treasure
Albert created, his pride, his vision.

President of the Royal Commission
That oversaw the Great Exhibition,
Albert was pivotal to its success.
He was elected Chancellor, no less,
Of Cambridge University. He found,
To his horror (he was on hostile ground),
That all they taught there was theology:
No moral sciences (philosophy),
Nor any political economy;
No natural sciences, no history;
No modern languages. It's a mystery
How this august seat of learning had the gall
To call itself a university at all.
Prince Albert changed all that. Radical reform:
Moral and natural sciences, the new norm.

His influence on the Queen was profound.
Victoria was on perilous ground.

Her fierce dislike of Tories was clear.
It was the Prince's particular fear
She was heading for a fall. Robert Peel
Was waiting in the wings. Melbourne's appeal
Was on the wane. When the dreaded time came,
The Queen must play the political game.
She could afford no favourites. She learned,
In time, before she had her fingers burned,
The need to remain above politics:
Power and prejudice – a lethal mix.

Family life

As a model husband, Albert excelled.
As the 'little wife', the Queen felt compelled
To defer to the Prince: in the upbringing
Of their family; in the daily running
Of their private household; in the managing
Of royal affairs; in short, in everything.
Devoted and loyal, she would do nothing,
Not choose a bonnet, nor move a photograph,
Without her husband's leave. Should we cry or laugh?

This was the role demanded of a wife.
It was a unique and challenging life
Being a Queen, but Albert's dominance
Was total. The Prince's pre-eminence,
As a husband, is what men expected.
He, in turn, was worshipped and respected.
He broke Victoria's will. His "dear child"
She became, submissive, trusting and mild.

Almost inevitably there were rows.
Within ten months of their marriage vows
Their first daughter was born, Victoria.
The new parents' joy and euphoria

Rhyming History

Were tempered by doubts, on the Prince's part,
On the subject of her care. A bad start.
Dr. Clark, in Albert's considered view,
The royal quack, had not the faintest clue.
The child was starving, Albert told the Queen.
Feed the infant or he would quit the scene.
"Take the child away and do what you like,"
Was his ultimatum. He was on strike!
"If she dies," (this was his final salvo)
"You will have it on your conscience." So,
This was how Albert asserted his will:
With threats and bombast. A most bitter pill.

Yet it seemed to work. The family grew,
Virtuous and dutiful through and through.
Nine children were born in seventeen years.
All survived to adulthood. There were tears,
There was stress, but this, self-evidently,
Was the perfect 'Victorian' family.

Victoria dreaded her pregnancies.
She confessed to detesting all babies,
Calling her offspring "froglike", if you please.
Infants were little better than a curse,
Distracting her attention (which was worse)
Away from her beloved husband. He,
The perfect papa in the nursery
And in the schoolroom, was a good parent,
Devoted to his children. A tyrant
Such a father would be accounted now.
Albert imposed an iron will, and how.

Poor little Vicky was whipped for lying,
Common practice, there is no denying,
But savage nonetheless. For discipline
Moulded the character. It was a sin
To spare the rod. Children should never win.

Yet Albert was a fine family man.
He played with his children, the rumour ran,
A rarity in those buttoned-up days.

In winter it was skates, sledges and sleighs,
Picnics in the long summer holidays,
And at Christmas the magnificent tree,
A custom imported from Germany
And enjoyed to this day. Thanks to the Prince,
This has blessed our Christmases ever since.

The end of Melbourne

The Melbourne government was on the ropes,
A sorry saga of muddle, dashed hopes
And internal dissent. The past two years
Had achieved little. Victoria's tears,

Rhyming History

As she bade farewell to her honest friend,
Were bitter, but the party had to end.
Awkward colleagues, Lord John Russell for one,
And the ever-troublesome Palmerston,
Were rocking the boat and, like it or not,
The PM himself was losing the plot.
He took to nodding off in Cabinet.

His government was not without merit.
Some welcomed the Education Act,
Others the Penny Post. It's a sad fact,
Nonetheless, that his lease had expired.
Poor old Melbourne was lazy and tired,
Faint-hearted to boot, it can't be denied.
Targeted by radicals on one side
And Tories on the other, he was lost.

Stubborn as a mule, this came at a cost.
For it was economics in the end
That brought him down. Never one to pretend
That he understood figures or detail,
He stuck to his guns, but was doomed to fail.
His final budget showed a deficit
Of millions. He was simply not fit,
For all his charm, intelligence and wit,
To hold office, that was the nub of it.

The Whigs were defeated on the budget.   **1841**
The game was finally up, this he knew,
Yet Melbourne was far from sure what to do.
His favoured option was to resign.
The Queen (and Russell) took a tougher line:
Soldier on! Melbourne bowed to their will,
But a further defeat, for good or ill,
Forced the old rogue's hand: dissolution,
The only sensible solution.

48

The Early Victorians

The election of August '41
Signalled a watershed, all said and done,
In British electoral history.
How so? No particular mystery.
For the first time a party in office
With a Commons majority (mark this)
Was dismissed, not by a disgruntled King –
In former times not an uncommon thing –
Nor even by a vote in Parliament,
But by the electorate, a clear statement
Of popular will (as far as it went).

Melbourne's Whigs suffered a crushing defeat.
The Tories were fairly swept off their feet,
So comprehensive was their victory:
A generous working majority
Of some eighty seats. By convention,
The Whigs stayed in office. The tension,
However, was low. Everyone knew
It was out with the old, in with the new.
A vote of no confidence turned the screw.
To widespread relief, not to sound unkind,
The discredited Whigs finally resigned.

Lord Melbourne's advice

Melbourne, to give the old buffer his due,
Counselled Victoria what she should do.
Peel was anathema to her, he knew,
So he steeled himself to prepare the ground
For the new PM. His logic was sound,
For Peel had the Queen's best interests at heart.
The pair had got off to a dreadful start
With the vexed 'Bedchamber Ladies' question,
Two years before. There was some suggestion
That this old dispute, bitter and heated,
Might now regrettably be repeated.

Rhyming History

The Viscount, with his customary tact,
Brokered a compromise, and that's a fact.
Prompted by Anson, Albert's secretary,
With the Prince's assent, almost certainly,
Melbourne held secret discussions with Peel.
He trod with care. How would Sir Robert feel
If just three ladies of the Queen's household
Resigned, thus releasing the stranglehold
Of the Whigs on the royal *entourage*?

This move proved acceptable, by and large,
To Peel (no cause for him now to back down)
And to the Prince, on behalf of the Crown.
Melbourne had useful advice too for Peel
On how to survive on an even keel
With the Queen. Don't talk *at* her, he advised;
Don't be too solemn; and don't be surprised
If she disapproves of your "Sunday face"!
In short, Melbourne counselled, know your place.

In turn he proffered advice to the Queen.
He urged tact. What did her ministers mean,
She asked (days after Melbourne had resigned),
By coming across as brash and unkind?
Melbourne was at a loss to hazard why,
Unless, of course, they felt awkward and shy.
If her Majesty failed to understand
Any measures that her ministers planned,
Or found herself disagreeing strongly,
Better to pause and, rightly or wrongly,
Take time for mature consideration.
His message was one of moderation,
And caution. His words of wisdom made sense,
Not least when he spoke of Albert's influence –
Not as an impediment, but as a boon.
The Prince had arrived not a moment too soon.

The Early Victorians

When Melbourne took final leave of the Queen,
Victoria wept, an affecting scene.
"We do and shall miss you so dreadfully,"
She wrote, but she recovered steadily.
Losing Melbourne was the saddest event
Of her life, yet he came to represent
The past. She was soon resigned to his loss.
The Tories, far from heralding chaos,
Ushered in an age of prosperity
And growth. Peel's much-admired dexterity
In matters fiscal brought security.
The Queen, as she grew in maturity,
Warmed to Sir Robert until, in the end,
She accounted him "a kind and true friend".

This was largely down to Albert. Reserved,
Hard-working and bright, Sir Robert deserved
The support and confidence of the Queen.
These he earned in spades. Who could have foreseen
The miraculous transformation
That in five short years shaped the nation,
All thanks to Peel's imagination,
Skill and iron determination?

Peel's inheritance

Britain stood at rock bottom. The budget,
However much the Whigs tried to fudge it,
Showed an accumulated deficit
Of seven and a half million pounds.
I am well aware the figure astounds.
Industry was stagnant; trade was depressed;
Factory workers were hungry and stressed.
In Paisley and Bolton thousands of folk
Survived on hand-outs, no word of a joke.
Bad harvests (the rains were unforgiving)
Had ratcheted up the cost of living

Rhyming History

To heights unsustainable for the poor.
Penury, pushing at an open door,
Fomented riots and social unrest.
If Melbourne had sought to rise to the test,
Posterity might have forgiven him.
He despised the poor. This was signally dim
In political terms, but worse, far worse,
Was his cold indifference. Melbourne I curse.

Such was the Tories' grim inheritance.
Peel was blessed with a rare intelligence,
Good sense and a wealth of experience.
Already PM for a hundred days
Under old King William, he won praise
For his cool head and his progressive ways.
That was a minority government,
But he paid William the compliment
Of stepping into the breach. A smart chap.

The Tories were firmly back on the map.
Peel had gained strength in opposition,
Consolidating his position
As a future candidate for PM.
Ready to engage, but slow to condemn,
He played his hand with *finesse.* Why worry
If the young Queen appeared in no hurry
To part with her fuddy-duddy old friend,
The lackadaisical Melbourne? His end
Was assured. Peel had been content to wait.
Only a strong electoral mandate
Tempted him to return to high office.

Far from regretting a poisoned chalice,
Peel relished the challenge. He knew the form:
Celebrated for root-and-branch reform
Of the criminal law during his years
As Home Secretary, despite the fears

Of diehards in the judiciary;
Fêted too, as Irish Secretary,
For the new Irish Constabulary
(Or 'Peelers'), the very first police force
In Britain; and later famous, of course,
For 'Bobbies', the Metropolitan Police.

These initiatives were all of a piece,
Calculated to promote the rule of law.
What else, Sir Robert asked, was government for?

Trade

Great Britain's dire economic plight
Called for a genius to set it right.
The problem, in a word, was poverty:
Spiralling prices, failing industry,

Rhyming History

Low wages – a broken economy.
The Prime Minister's chosen remedy
Was not to give succour to the Chartists,
Forever shouting and shaking their fists;
Nor to subject the textile factories
To reduced hours; nor even, by degrees,
To amend the iniquitous Poor Laws.
No. Peel announced, after a decent pause,
That trade was the key. Liberalise trade.
Cut tariffs across the board. The case was made.

The best strategy for helping the poor
Was to lower the price of goods. Therefore,
Peel argued, cut tariffs on the imports
On which they relied – on stuff of all sorts,
Not just food, but the products on which they,
Or their masters, depended, a clear way
Of reducing prices and costs. Well, hey,
That sounds pretty simple, wouldn't you say?

Yes… except… the government's revenue
Would fall at a stroke. Tariffs were the glue
That held the economy together.
To cut tariffs in inclement weather
Was downright folly. It was just not done.
Was Sir Robert Peel really the one
To reverse the trend and fly in the face
Of accepted practice? What a disgrace!
Slash tariffs by all means, but avoid it
If it meant running up a deficit.

To stimulate trade, tariffs must be cut.
Upon this point Peel was adamant, but –
And it was a big 'but' – the deficit
Had to be addressed. No bottomless pit
Was acceptable, no backlog of debt.
A surplus was sought and targets were set.

Taxation

To bridge the revenue gap, income tax
Was a considered option. Mind your backs!
A tax levied only in time of war
Would cause an outcry: stealth by the back door.
Yet Peel's peacetime budget of '42   **1842**
Revived the income tax. Sir Robert knew,
If only from a fiscal point of view,
That this was something he needed to do.
The figure fixed, after earnest debate,
Was sevenpence in the pound (a flat rate).

A generous exemption limit
Softened the blow. The running deficit
Would be extinguished as the income tax
Yielded (allowing Britain to relax)
Some four million pounds, with a surplus –
Simply achieved without trouble or fuss –
Of up to two million to apply
To tariff reform. Few folk could deny
Peel's triumph. Consumers reaped the reward,
As tariffs were lowered across the board:
On raw materials to five *per cent*;
On foreign factory goods (Heaven-sent)
To some twenty *per cent*. Export duties –
This was one of the budget's true beauties –
Were also reduced. An added bonus
Was that Peel still predicted a surplus
Of five hundred thousand pounds for the year.

Even the Whigs managed to raise a cheer.
"All the time he was speaking," one remarked,
Despite the dissent that the budget sparked,
"One felt 'Thank God Peel is Minister'." Well,
So much for Sir Robert's fiscal bombshell.

Rhyming History

The Corn Laws

Not everyone was happy. Let's pause
To take a look at the dreaded Corn Laws.

The saga began in 1815.
Farming was in crisis. Picture the scene.
Agriculture, under terrible strain,
Suffered from the import of foreign grain.
The end of the Napoleonic wars,
With the revival of trade, was one cause.
This, and a series of awful harvests,
Threatened the great landowners' interests.
Domestic producers bore huge losses.
Poor relief, one of the many crosses
Farmers had to bear, also played a part.
The outlook was dire. Where does one start?

The Corn Laws were passed to alleviate,
With urgency and haste, the depressed state
Of British agriculture. Why the panic?
The price of corn had halved! The mood was manic.

Relief was absolutely necessary
To deliver the rural economy
From ruin. The Corn Laws sought to stabilise
The price of wheat. It will come as no surprise
To learn that farmers sought to keep prices high –
Higher than was possible to justify,
At least when grain imported from abroad
Came in at a price the poor could afford.

Eighty shillings (per quarter) was the price set –
More than most farmers could ever hope to get –
Before corn was allowed to be imported.
Efforts to set a lower rate were thwarted.

The Early Victorians

William Cobbett spoke out against the Law.
He firmly believed there was trouble in store.
He was right. The domestic monopoly
In corn adversely affected industry.
As the cost of food increased, so consumers
Had less to spend. There were worrying rumours
That the poor were struggling to stay alive.
While families all needed bread to survive,
The price was kept artificially high.

The level of scandal was hard to deny.
Over the years ministers sought to apply,
To soften the blow, a sort of sliding scale,
Over-sophisticated and sure to fail.

It was quite complicated, but here goes.
As the market rate for home-grown corn rose,
Imports were permitted, but at a price –
Effectively a tariff. In a trice,
Ministers hoped, fairness would be achieved.
Extremes of poverty would be relieved
As the cost of bread, to some degree, fell.

Flexibility was all very well,
But farmers were against a sliding scale,
Intrusive and complex, beyond the pale.
Zealous free traders, on the other hand,
For reasons not that hard to understand,
Disparaged the wretched scale as a fudge.
Unlikely it was that either would budge.

The bitter debate rumbled on for years.
The indolent Lord Melbourne, it appears,
Hoped the problem would simply go away.
Corn Law reform? He lived from day to day.
The whole thing bored him to stupefaction.
Once, when he did decide on some action,

With the full agreement of his Cabinet,
He called after them: "Stop a bit! I forget…
"What did we agree? To lower the price
"Of bread… or not?" Let this alone suffice
To prove Melbourne manifestly unfit
For office. Little of use or profit
Did he achieve, that's the sad truth of it.

The Corn Laws *versus* free trade

What is more disappointing, however,
Is that Peel, sophisticated, clever
And politically astute, was slow
To take a lead. The stubborn so-and-so
Was the strongest advocate of free trade
(This we have seen) and yet no case was made,
In his modest view, for Corn Law reform.
As a Tory, of course, this was the norm –
The party of the landed interest.
Would it help the farmer? That was the test.

Sir Robert was shortly to cause a storm
By changing his mind. The case for reform
Was overwhelming. Yet every year,
Until '45, he would raise a cheer
By solidly voting against repeal.
His *volte-face*, when it came, took nerves of steel.
Shifting his ground held no terrors for Peel.

Richard Cobden and John Bright

The Anti-Corn Law League was going strong
By 1841. It was quite wrong,
Argued its founder, one Richard Cobden,
The best and most single-minded of men,
To punish the poor with expensive bread.
A sober sort of fellow, no hothead,

The Early Victorians

He advocated low taxes, free trade
And peace. No progress would ever be made
Unless these three key objectives were met.
He despised the aristocratic set.
It was leaders of trade and industry
Who should, by rights, be running the country.

No orator, he argued cogently
For Corn Law reform. It's no mystery
How he achieved his ends. Hard graft and drive
Kept the hopes and dreams of the League alive.
His fund-raising skills were legendary.
Cobden understood, better than many,
That spreading the word was what mattered most.
Thanks to the railways and the Penny Post,
Pamphlets were distributed far and wide,
Giving the people a chance to decide.
Cobden, a man of simple common sense,
Ensured the League steered clear of violence.
That, at least, was his avowed policy.

In '41 he became an MP.
His influence grew proportionately,
But he never lost his integrity.
He remained detached, no party man he.
Corn Law repeal was Cobden's victory –
Not only the verdict of history,
But that of Sir Robert Peel. In his eyes,
Cobden took top honours. This caused surprise,
Given the vehemence of his attacks
On good Sir Robert over tariffs and tax.

Another leading figure was John Bright.
A compelling speaker, blunt and forthright,
Cobden had recruited him to the cause.
"Oaks," John averred, "were never felled with straws."

He had a way with words. Landlords, he cried,
Were snatching the food "that God had supplied"
From the mouths of the poor. What oratory!

Bright complemented Cobden to a T.
When the League celebrated victory,
A great procession marched through Rochdale
Bearing a loaf baked on a massive scale.
Two names were emblazoned on its sides: 'Bright'
And 'Cobden'. They must have done something right.

Alongside his budget of '42,
Peel introduced a new Corn Law. He knew,
In his heart, this measure was not enough –
A modest move, but only standard stuff.
He tinkered with the famous 'sliding scale'.
The so-called 'Leaguers' fought him tooth and nail.

The Early Victorians

There were stormy meetings throughout the land,
Where effigies of Peel, I understand,
Were burnt in public, leading to arrests.
Well, so much for Cobden's peaceful protests.
Tories in Parliament made it clear
They wanted *more* protection. Oh, dear.
The matter was fudged for another year,
As the House of Commons approved the Bill.
Reform was to prove a most bitter pill.

Poor relief

Violence was in the air. '42
Was a dangerous year. What do you do
When 17,000 folk in Paisley –
Destitute (let nobody say lazy) –
Were at risk of starving by slow degrees,
Literally thousands of families?
Peel and the Queen herself, amazingly,
Through a General Relief Committee,
Stepped up to assist the poor and hungry.
The Queen gave five hundred pounds, a vast sum.
Donations from the rich were welcome.
This Victoria wrote in a letter
To be read out in church. What way better,
Argued Peel, for the Queen to save the day?

A smart move by her Maj, I have to say.
Folk took note of this show of sympathy
For the poor, depressed people of Paisley.
She encouraged Paisley shawls to be worn
At Court – all down to a shortage of corn!

The relief was an interim measure.
Peel had no intention whatever
Of creating any sort of welfare state,
A notion too awful to contemplate.

But he felt for the poor, that's very clear,
Social unrest his particular fear.
His trump card in the war on poverty
Was free trade. No one knew better than he
The value of a strong economy.
The Corn Laws were a strange anomaly,
At odds with Peel's overall policy
Of tariff reform. When push comes to shove,
Let a man change his mind! Heavens above!
Peel acquitted himself as he thought fit.
The Laws were repealed and the Tories split.

Tax, protests and riots

I'm running ahead. Back to '42.
Peel's fiscal reforms were slow to work through.
The new income tax, as you might expect,
Took time to set up and months to collect.
In August the crisis came to a head,
With dozens of rioters left for dead.
The Staffordshire colliers went on strike.
Unemployed workers and rebels alike
Disabled the steam engines in the pits,
Pulling the boiler plugs from their sockets
And breaking machinery into bits.
Mill-hands, armed to the teeth with pikes and flails,
Pitchforks and bludgeons studded with nails,
Threatened the peace. Workhouses were attacked,
The private houses of magistrates sacked,
And factories looted and burned. Cheshire,
The Potteries, Shropshire and Lancashire –
The northern heartlands, all were on fire!

Even Drayton Manor, Peel's country seat
Up in Staffordshire, was feeling the heat.
The house was armed (all top secret, of course) –
Peel feared his home could be taken by force.

The Early Victorians

Not so Lady Julia! An attack,
If ever it came, would be driven back.
"No man actually attacking doors
"And windows," she cried, to rousing applause,
"Would have left this place alive." Good for her!
A marauding horde? The odd saboteur?
No bother! A general's daughter she,
Julia played her part vigorously.

Peel performed on the national stage
With equal aplomb. In a state of rage,
The country was volatile, dangerous
And raw. For cool, Sir Robert was famous.
While waiting for his tax reforms to work,
Strong measures were called for. Peel did not shirk.
The anniversary of Peterloo,
Alas, loomed large. The Prime Minister knew
That in Manchester this carried the risk
Of riotous assembly. Peel was brisk.
The massacre was marked, every year,
By demonstrations. Sir Robert's fear,
In a summer of seething discontent,
Was that this highly-charged, angry event
Could trigger uproar on a deadly scale.

Guards were despatched to Manchester by rail.
From Windsor, a Royal Proclamation
Was issued to a restless nation.
Subjects were warned that breaches of the peace
Would not go unpunished. Riots must cease.
Tumultuous meetings and assemblies
Were banned forthwith. The force of these decrees
Was immediate. The authorities,
Reeling from a crisis of confidence,
Recovered their nerve. Manchester saw sense.
There were no fatalities. Peel's tough stance
Steadied the buffs. By a tragic mischance,

Troops at Preston were forced to open fire.
The death toll would certainly have been higher
Had not Peel been so focused and robust.
His foresight turned the tide, but only just.

Gradual recovery

The budget of May 1843   **1843**
Sent out mixed signals. A recovery?
The long-suffering people of Paisley
Saw unemployment falling in the town.
Demand for poor relief was also down.
Yet economic prospects were still bleak.
Returns from customs and excise were weak.
The dreaded income tax had yielded less
Than Peel had hoped. An improvement? Well, yes…
But progress was sluggish and perilous.
Instead of the much heralded surplus,
The budget showed a stubborn deficit:
Two million pounds! Calls for Peel to quit,
Vocal on all fronts, fell on stony ground.
Sir Robert's fiscal policies were sound.
He stuck to his guns, steady and composed.
"If the income tax had not been imposed,"
He asked the Commons, "where would we be now?"
There was no alternative, anyhow.
Melbourne had failed. The country needed Peel,
His incisive mind and his nerves of steel.

Assassination

Peel was exposed to personal danger.
One terrible day a total stranger
Shot and killed his Private Secretary –
A case of mistaken identity.
Edward Drummond, murdered at Charing Cross,
Had recently accompanied his boss

To Scotland. Peel had travelled with the Queen,
In her carriage, while Drummond was seen
Travelling in Sir Robert's private coach.
The conduct of both was beyond reproach,
But MacNaghten, the wretched assassin,
Noted the coach poor Drummond had sat in
And marked the fellow out as Sir Robert.

England was suddenly on high alert –
Too late for Dummond, alas. The good Queen
Condemned MacNaghten's trial as obscene.
He pleaded insanity. The outrage
This caused the Queen fairly flies off the page.
To allow "the verdict of *Not Guilty*,"
She wrote, "on account of *Insanity*"
Clearly drove her Majesty to despair.
MacNaghten was "conscious and aware".
Relaxed as ever, Peel was less concerned.
He still walked home, so Victoria learned,
From the Commons alone. She disapproved,
But brave Sir Robert refused to be moved.

Lady Julia, sadly, was hard hit
By Drummond's death. She had a nervous fit.
Months it took her to recover from it.
Was this the heroine who resisted
The Drayton insurgents and insisted
On defending her home with all her might?

The Queen visits Drayton

In November, to Sir Robert's delight,
He welcomed Victoria and Albert
As his guests to Drayton. A clear convert,
The Queen had overcome her prejudice
And warmed to Peel. The 'bedchamber' crisis

Rhyming History

Was long forgotten. Sir Robert worked hard,
And with subtlety, to win her regard.
When he proposed a Royal Commission
On Fine Arts, Peel sought the Queen's permission
To invite young Prince Albert to head it –
Blatant flattery (there, I have said it),
But a smart choice. In his own quiet way,
Peel urged the Queen to give Albert a say
In the nation's affairs. To this day,
We have cause to be grateful. Witness this:
England stood on the edge of the abyss.
This Albert saw. Poverty, injustice,
Unemployment… These had to be addressed.

On his visit to Drayton (I'm impressed)
He took time out to tour the factories
In nearby Birmingham. There, if you please,
He was greeted by the Chartist Mayor,
A hosier by trade. Peel was aware
Of the risk, but gave the trip his blessing.
Some might have found the tour depressing.
Not Albert! He took a keen interest
In industry. Royalty at its best.

Peel reported that the visit passed off
With a level of success (now, don't scoff)
Most striking "amid all the discontent
"And disloyalty". By common consent,
This would have been the first royal walkabout.
It gave the people plenty to talk about.

Victoria and the Prince took the train
From Watford. I ought perhaps to explain:
The royal coach boarded the train with them!
It disembarked at Tamworth (no problem),
Whence the party proceeded to Drayton.
Guests included the Duke of Wellington

The Early Victorians

And old William's widow, Adelaide.
Of the myriad of compliments paid,
Peel would most have treasured that of the Queen.
Drayton Manor, she told Lord Aberdeen,
Of all the houses she had ever seen,
Was the most comfortable. Praise indeed.
Modern plumbing answered every need,
As did the exquisite upholstery
And lavish furnishings. One novelty,
The central heating, was a royal 'first'.
Sir Robert, we're told, was proud fit to burst.

Chatsworth

To make their historic journey complete,
The couple drove to Chatsworth, country seat
Of the 6th Duke of Devonshire. Albert
Told Anson, who told Peel (this must have hurt),
That he counted Chatsworth the finest place
He had yet seen in England. To Peel's face
The Prince would doubtless have been more discreet.
There were half a dozen oxen to eat,
Some two hundred gallons of ale to drink,
And as for the gardens (what do you think?)
Thousands of lanterns to light up the trees,
With fireworks to crown the festivities.

Joseph Paxton arranged this great display.
The most gifted gardener of his day,
This fellow let nothing stand in his way.
The Duke spotted the genius in him
And appointed young Joseph, on a whim,
His head gardener, aged just twenty-three.
He repaid the Duke's trust, believe you me.
He built a giant conservatory,
In glass, and a stupendous rockery.

He designed a fountain, to great applause,
From water piped from the neighbouring moors.
Mark this: "I should have liked that man of yours
"For one of my generals." Who said it?
The Duke of Wellington, to his credit.

Paxton's hour had come. The time was ripe.
The 'Great Stove', so-called, was the prototype
For the Crystal Palace which made his name.
Three cheers for 'Sir' Joseph, as Paxton became.

Better economic news

Towards the end of this pivotal year,
The picture improved. The message was clear.
Trade was on the up. Even income tax
Was subject to fewer bitter attacks.

With rising demand, chiefly for cotton,
The deficit was all but forgotten.
The mills in the north were busy again,
As folk had more to spend. The trend was plain.
The Prime Minister's fiscal policy
Was working its magic. Prosperity
Beckoned. Peel, in the space of three short years,
Had saved the nation. Blood, sweat and tears
(That infamous trio) had been the price,
But bold Sir Robert had broken the ice.

Soon he was pushing at an open door.
The abundant harvest of '44   **1844**
Wrong-footed opponents of the Corn Laws,
Who had little choice but to take a pause.
The respite was short. There was grief ahead.
But Peel, for now, could sleep soundly in bed.

The railways

The Queen loved travelling on the railway,
The swiftest mode of transport of the day.
The age of the train was well under way
By the time Victoria came to the throne,
But 'Victorians' made the railways their own.

The first steam engine, in 1803,
Had been used in a Welsh colliery
To pull pit wagons along a tracked route.
Coal mines in the north quickly followed suit.
Steam locomotives, some ninety or so,
Were widely used in the pits (this we know)
By the eighteen-twenties. It needed brains
To leap from these trucks to passenger trains.

It took no time at all. A first survey
For the Stockton and Darlington Railway

Rhyming History

Was made in July 1821
By budding engineer George Stephenson,
Assisted by his eighteen-year-old son,
Robert. The new 'Stockton and Darlington'
Was designed to connect collieries
Near Bishop Auckland to the River Tees,
At Stockton. Driven by George Stephenson,
Their purpose-built engine, *Locomotion*,
A machine of unprecedented power,
Attained speeds of twenty-four miles per hour.
Its purpose was to carry coal and flour.
This it achieved with conspicuous success,
Transporting a load of eighty tons, no less,
In two hours over a distance of nine miles.
Little wonder the Stephensons were all smiles.

Passenger trains

For the future, more significant by far
Was the attachment of a passenger car,
Named *The Experiment*. This was the true star!
A cross between a shed and a caravan,
It was not what it looked like, but how it ran.
So the age of passenger traffic began.

It was not until 1825
That the Stockton and Darlington 'went live'.
Four years it took from that early survey
To do the job, a mere trice I should say,
Given the colossal undertaking.
The Stephensons, there was no mistaking,
Were the leading pioneers of the age.
They even established the standard gauge,
Four feet, eight and a half inches. Brunel
Built to a broader gauge but, sad to tell,
This led to massive inconvenience.
Different widths simply didn't make sense.

The Early Victorians

When railways laid to varying gauges met,
For the first time, at Gloucester, the stage was set
For chaos and confusion. All very strange –
A sudden and most unwelcome interchange!
Disgruntled, angry passengers, long delays,
Lost luggage… A throwback to the bad old days,
Not what folk were expecting from the railways.

The 1846 Gauge of Railways Act
Favoured the Stephensons' gauge and that's a fact,
Chiefly because there were miles and miles of track
Already laid, and there was no going back.

In terms of speed and efficiency,
Locomotives were in their infancy.
Were steam-powered engines up to the task
Of passenger transport? Well, since you ask,
Investors were far from wild about steam,
Despite the success of the leading team,
George Stephenson and Son. It was their dream
To prove conclusively that steam was best.
In '29 they were put to the test.

The Liverpool and Manchester Railway
Was in prospect. The board brooked no delay
In their quest for a suitable engine –
But steam or horse power? Where to begin?
Frankly, they were in a bit of a spin,
Until one of the directors proposed…
A trial. None of his colleagues was opposed.

Stephenson's *Rocket*

A competition was organised
For the best steam engine. Few were surprised
When Robert Stephenson entered the ring.
His *Rocket*, so-called, was a wondrous thing.

Rhyming History

Before an eager ten thousand-strong crowd,
George Stephenson's son did his father proud.
Their family-designed locomotive
Covered the sixty-mile course, as I live,
At an astonishing average speed
Of fourteen m.p.h. All were agreed
That the *Rocket* was the winner. *Cyclops*,
Powered by horses, was one of the flops.
Sans Pareil was found to be overweight,
While *Novelty* broke down, such was her fate.

The board purchased the *Rocket*. Well, why not?
The locomotive took off like a shot.
Robert did not rest on his laurels. No,
The project still had a long way to go.
He perfected his craft. Larger, stronger
His engines became, smarter and longer.

So the reign of the Stephensons began.
They exported steam engines to Milan,
To Paris, Berlin and St. Petersburg.
I know this may sound a little absurd,
But all their engines were built at Forth Street,
Newcastle, in their own workshops. Some feat,
Given that the work was all done by hand,
Without one single crane, I understand.

Robert Stephenson was chief engineer
On a vast range of schemes – as pioneer,
Designer, political lobbyist,
Bridge builder, surveyor… you get the gist.
Add 'project manager' to this long list
And the picture is complete. For its day,
Robert's London and Birmingham Railway
Was a monumental undertaking:
Strategic planning, finance, surveying

The Early Victorians

(He walked the route six times), a huge work force
Of 20,000 men – nothing, of course,
Compared to the technical expertise
Required of the builder. Skills such as these
Guaranteed the line's success. 'Delegate'
Was Stephenson's watchword. Some six months late
(A trifle), the first train bound for London,
In all its glory, steamed into Euston.
Sorry, I forgot to tell you the date:
The new station opened in '38.

The battle for economy was lost:
Fifty thousand pounds per mile the line cost,
Well over twice the figure projected,
As shocking as it was unexpected.
Yet the profits from the great enterprise
Took even hardened cynics by surprise.

Rhyming History

The railways were here to stay. Investment
For the future was assured, testament
To the talents of chaps like Stephenson.
The case for steam was conclusively won.

As a bridge builder, Stephenson excelled.
Doubts as to his expertise were expelled
By his amazing bridge across the Tyne,
At Newcastle, in 1849.
This was formally opened by the Queen,
The most impressive she had ever seen.
The Royal Border Bridge across the Tweed
Also caught Victoria's eye. Indeed,
Its twenty-eight arch viaduct of stone
Was the toast of Berwick. It stood alone.

Not all Stephenson's projects succeeded.
In '47, if proof were needed,
His bridge across the River Dee gave way
Under a passenger train. Sad to say,
Five poor folk perished. The locomotive
Just made it, but the train sank like a sieve.
The cause of the disaster, it appears,
Was strain on the cast-iron girders. Fears,
Naturally, that Robert was to blame
Would forever be a blot on his name.
He looked haggard and pale at the inquest,
Fearing a manslaughter verdict at best.
This could not be dismissed as a mishap.

He was ready, it seems, to take the rap,
But the verdict that the jury returned
Was accidental death. Stephenson learned
From the awfulness of this experience.
A fellow of honesty and plain good sense,
He refused to risk losing another train
And never used cast-iron girders again.

The Early Victorians

Brunel

Isambard Kingdom Brunel – a great name!
The origin of 'Isambard', some claim,
Is Germanic. This sounds exactly right,
Given that '*Eisenbart*' means 'iron-bright'.
For, as a mechanical engineer,
Brunel was the best, outclassing his peer
(And friendly rival), Robert Stephenson.

A driven soul, whose work was never done,
Brunel once kept a twenty-hour day,
Over six weeks, to complete his survey
Of what became the Great Western Railway.

His father was an engineering great.
It was little Isambard's happy fate
To follow in his footsteps. Aged just four,
The prodigy learned to observe… and draw.
He mastered Euclidean geometry
By the age of eight and was quick to see,
One year later, the imminent collapse
Of a new build. Beginner's luck, perhaps?
Not so. He fulfilled his early promise
In spades, excelling as an apprentice
To a master clockmaker in Paris
And then as an assistant engineer –
A young man still, in his twentieth year –
In his father's boldest undertaking,
A tunnel from Rotherhithe to Wapping,
Running under the River Thames, no less.

The project met with setbacks, I confess,
With serious incidents of flooding.
For years the enterprise came to nothing.
Two miners were drowned in one accident,
Engulfed in filthy water, sediment

Rhyming History

And heavy sludge. Young Isambard dived in
To help others, heedless of his own skin.

The youth himself went on to greater things,
But the Thames Tunnel nonetheless grew wings.
It opened at last, officially,
After lengthy delays, in '43.
The Queen and Albert came to take a look,
A compliment rare in anyone's book.
For the Thames Tunnel, for all its delays,
Was a true marvel. In its early days
Only foot passengers were allowed through,
Until '65, when out of the blue
It was purchased, in its entirety,
By the East London Railway Company.

Railways, of course, were all the rage by then,
And the Thames Tunnel scored ten out of ten.
Two hundred thousand the company paid,
A vast sum, and a good profit they made.
Once the conversion work had been done,
The East London Railway, second to none,
Established a service for Londoners
That proved one of the capital's wonders.
The line, to this day, is still going strong.
I am sure you'll correct me if I'm wrong,
But it now serves the London Overground.
In the *A to Z* it's easily found.

Brunel's achievements

Five feet, four inches tall, neat as a pin,
A slave to order and to discipline,
Isambard was a human dynamo.
He always had a cigar on the go
And wore a distinctive stove-pipe top hat,
In which he kept his papers. I like that!

Known as the 'Little Giant', Brunel
Was destined for greatness, as time would tell.

He designed the Clifton Suspension Bridge,
In Bristol. His legendary courage
Was amply demonstrated one fine day.
Hoisted in a basket, as was his way,
High in the air above the Avon Gorge,
The cable got all tangled up. By George!
It was a long way down. What did he do?
He doffed his hat and without further ado
Shinned up the rope and disentangled it.
Athletic and nimble, fearless and fit,
Brunel rescued himself… and his basket.

Rhyming History

Isambard's structure had the longest span
Of any bridge so far known to man:
Seven hundred and two feet. I'm a fan.
Thomas Telford had rubbished Brunel's plan,
Submitting his own proposals instead.
Thomas's fame must have gone to his head.
He was overruled by a committee
Which favoured Brunel unanimously.

Work began on the bridge in '31,
But political riots in Clifton
Led to investors withdrawing their cash.
Pressing on was considered far too rash,
So the project was abandoned for years –
Over thirty, to be precise. Three cheers,
I declare, for Isambard, even though
Some critics who claim to be in the know
Suggest that his original designs
Were updated along more modern lines.

The astonishing Brunel's claim to fame,
His finest and the one that made his name,
Was the Great Western Railway, a project
That Isambard relished, as you'd expect.
He even permitted himself to dream
Of an extension (also by steam)
From Bristol, can you believe, to New York!
This crazy idea was more than mere talk.
The *Great Western*, launched in '37,
Over two hundred feet long, great Heaven,
Was the largest steamship of her day.
Atlantic crossings were here to stay.
Seventy-four trips the *Great Western* made,
The first transatlantic passenger trade.

Back to the railway: London to the west!
Brunel was ready and rose to the test.

The Early Victorians

A bridge over the Thames at Maidenhead
He designed, the largest span, it is said,
For a brick arch bridge, which is what he chose.
This greatest of engineering heroes
Let nothing stand in his way. From London –
Or, more accurately, from Paddington –
The new railway ran (following the sun)
As far, in the first instance, as Bristol.

The project sadly took a deadly toll.
At Box, near Bath, a hundred lives were lost
In excavations, a terrible cost.
When he knew a tunnel had to be cut,
Was Isambard daunted? Anything but.
The tunnel measured three hundred yards long,
Dug through oolite rock. Brunel was on song.
Its capstone arches and fine balustrades
Are superb. Tunnels apart, tranquil glades,
Fresh woods and green pastures, all were destroyed –
The landed gentry were highly annoyed –
As the railway ploughed through the countryside.

Ruin and havoc, it can't be denied,
But these fine Victorian engineers
Were to overcome the landowners' fears
(To some degree) with the wonderful range,
And beauty, of their work. It may seem strange,
But their groundbreaking designs, embankments,
Cuttings, viaducts, bridges – monuments,
All, to the age of steam – in their own way
Enhance the landscape of Britain today.

There were more bizarre worries. The Provost
Of Eton feared the battle would be lost
For his pupils' morals should the railway
Come to Windsor. Brunel, without delay,

Rhyming History

Re-routed the line to take it through Slough.
The Provost's concerns raise a wry smile now,
But imagine the awful damage done
Had boys been free to hop up to London,
By train, to indulge in a 'bit of fun'.

Farmers were frightened that their crops would fry,
Set alight as the engines thundered by.
Their sensitive livestock, moved to panic,
Would take to the hills, moody and manic.

On Isambard's patch, from London to the west,
His broad gauge was still permitted, no contest.
He persisted, for the Great Western Railway,
To use his seven-foot track. In his heyday
Brunel had few rivals as an engineer.

Yet this wider gauge in the long term, I fear,
Was doomed. Years after his untimely demise,
Parliament decreed, to no one's surprise,
That all Isambard's rails, wherever they lay,
Should convert to standard. To widespread dismay?

On the contrary, it seems. Over one weekend,
In 1892, the broad gauge met its end.
Armies of navvies, in the space of just two days,
Lifted the track and replaced it! Beyond all praise.

Isambard's buildings were intriguing too.
His Bristol Temple Meads, though spanking new,
Was the most atypical of stations.
Its medieval crenellations
And its four-square structure made it look less
Like a rail terminus than a fortress,
A cross between a college and a castle.
Brunel, perhaps, was a bit of a rascal.

The Early Victorians

He challenged the public with his designs,
Witty and inventive, one of the signs
Of true genius. One instance, we're told,
Was the Box Tunnel. Brunel was so bold
As to align it, deliberately,
So that the rising sun, for all to see,
Shone all the way through it on his birthday!
True or false? I could not possibly say.

Isambard Kingdom Brunel, aged fifty-three,
Died in 1859. Take it from me,
He was a burnt-out case. Fellows such as he
Give all to their work and die tragically.
He lost his life after suffering a stroke.

Robert Stephenson, this no word of a joke,
Within a month of Brunel's untimely death,
As if in sympathy, drew his final breath.
Given Robert's equal dedication,
Few were surprised. He found his vocation
And, like Brunel, his competitor and friend,
Pursued it at all costs to the bitter end.

Stephenson rests in Westminster Abbey.
Why not Brunel? Decidedly shabby.
Isambard does get a window, it's true –
Altered and moved in 1952 –
Erected on the north side of the nave,
In 1868. But Brunel's grave
Is in the Kensal Green Cemetery.
Interred with the rest of his family,
This is where Isambard preferred to be.
There are numerous statues of Brunel.
The one at Temple serves him very well.
There is, appropriately, at Euston
A splendid one of Robert Stephenson.

Rhyming History

Growth of the railways

The railway network expanded apace.
Ninety-seven miles of track were in place
In 1830, but by '45
The system had gone into overdive.
Some two-and-a-half thousand miles of track
Had been opened. There was no looking back.
Thirty million passengers a year
Were travelling! Was this the end? No fear.
By the 1890s, I swear to you,
There were nineteen thousand miles of track. True.

Greater social mobility, too,
Was facilitated by the railways.
Day trips, well-earned family holidays,
Were suddenly within the means of most.
Organised excursions to the coast
Were all the rage. In 1851,
The year of the Great Exhibition,
Millions travelled by train to London
From far and wide. It was all rather fun.

The carriage of freight, all said and done,
Generated most of the revenue,
But all the established companies knew
That their respective reputations
Depended on the expectations
Of their passengers. Comfort, safety, speed
And price were paramount, all were agreed.
The Railway Act of 1844
Pegged Third Class fares (a free-for-all before)
At one penny a mile. Still dear, I'd say –
Too much for the poor and needy to pay.

Until the Railway Act, Third Class had no roof.
What did they think? Passengers were waterproof?

Nor were there any seats. Huddled together,
Travellers suffered, in dreadful weather,
Jostled and buffeted about. 'Standipedes'
These open wagons were called. Passengers' needs
Counted for little in those early days.

Second Class, whatever anyone says,
Enjoyed higher standards – seating, no less.
Not as comfy as First Class, I confess,
Where the seats were of horsehair. Second Class?
Their seats were wooden, a pain in the arse
(Pardon my French). The first lavatories
Appeared in trains in the 1860s,
Sleeping cars in the early '70s,
And diners as soon as '79.
The great steam engines roared along the line

Rhyming History

At seventy miles per hour or more.
By the end of the century steam, for sure,
Had transformed the landscape. (I'm sorry I swore).

Thomas Cook's popular excursions

It also gave birth to the package tour.
One summer's day, in 1841,
Thomas Cook, as a harmless bit of fun,
Organised an outing, on the railway,
From Leicester to Loughborough. For the day,
Inclusive of food (they had to be fed),
The round trip cost just a shilling a head.
The party numbered close on five hundred
And by all accounts was a huge success.
Cook arranged the jaunt with skill and *finesse.*

It set him thinking. The popular press
Were extolling the virtues of the train.
Rail travel was a pleasure, in the main,
But was apt to cause a measure of strain
In the planning. Where to go..? How to book..?
How much would it all cost..? Leave it to Cook!
Within four years of his Loughborough trip,
He had given up his job (no hardship)
To devote himself to his new career
As a holiday travel pioneer.

Thomas was teetotal and a Baptist.
An opportunity not to be missed
Was to encourage folk to go abroad,
At attractive prices most could afford,
As ambassadors for peace. No more war!
New people to meet! New worlds to explore!
Cook's original tours were far from grand.
Learning his trade, he focused on Scotland
And destinations, I understand,

The Early Victorians

In the West Country: seaside holidays,
Weekend excursions or longer stays.
He negotiated with the railways
For block bookings at favourable rates.
Cook meant business. He was one of the greats.

A fully researched itinerary,
Up-to-the-minute efficiency
And guaranteed reliability –
These were his strengths, you can take it from me.

It was not long before Cook took a chance,
Organising cheap passages to France.
Italy was next. He was well content
To press further into the Continent
With his 'Grand Circular Tour', so-called.
The snobs, it has to be said, were appalled.
"Riff-raff be damned!" cried the privileged few.
Switzerland… Austria… Germany, too…
The middle classes got everywhere!
Cue: horror, dismay and abject despair.

The Middle East was next. In '69,
Who do you reckon was standing in line
When the Suez Canal was opened? Cook!
A mark of honour in anyone's book.
Thomas, of course, hadn't pitched up alone.
Surrounded he was by tourists – his own!

Egypt… Palestine… Cook travelled in style.
He advertised pleasure trips down the Nile –
Indeed, he purchased an exclusive right
To these river trips. His margins were tight,
But his expertise and will to succeed
Meant a healthy profit was guaranteed.
Monopoly power! Such was his fame
That 'Cook's Canal' the Nile quickly became.

Rhyming History

Was there no end to what this man could do?
A jaunt round the world in '72
Set the seal on his reputation.

Every route and destination
Were the subject of his keen scrutiny.
Disappointment? God forbid! Mutiny?
Heaven forfend! Cook took such tender care
Of his troops he could send them anywhere:
Booted and spurred, over rugged terrain,
Through choppy waters, they'd never complain.

Two hundred and twenty-two days it took
To make it round the globe, all down to Cook.
Precursor of the package tour today,
From Rome to New York, from Nice to Bombay,
From Luxor to Bonn, good for Cook, I say.

The Early Victorians

Peel and Ireland

We'll leave Thomas and his tourists at play.
Back to politics. Peel, I understand,
Was directing his thoughts towards Ireland.
There was fresh trouble brewing, he believed.

Irish Catholics were sorely aggrieved.
In the governing of their proud nation,
Eighty *per cent* of the population
Had no influence. The Lord Lieutenant,
Appointed by the British government
And, as you might expect, a Protestant,
Enjoyed sweeping powers of patronage.
It would be little less than an outrage,
In the opinion of Lord de Grey
(The said Lieutenant), to fritter away
Key posts in the Irish judiciary,
The civil service and the military
On Catholics. Peel was far from impressed.
Time out of mind he tried his level best
To urge upon de Grey another test:
Not religion, but ability.

Sir Robert had the common sense to see
That his Lordship's benighted policy
Was fuelling anger and hostility
Among the Irish. Nationalism
Cast a dark shadow. Dissent and schism
Were sinister forces stalking the land.

Daniel O'Connell was taking a stand.
His Repeal Association, so-called,
Was on the march. Lately the movement had stalled,
But O'Connell, as outspoken as ever,
Was demanding change. Daniel was clever.

Rather than seek a final break with Britain,
He argued that the Act of 1801
Should be repealed to a limited extent.
The Irish should have back their Parliament,
But remain under the Crown. Well, fair enough.
Why not? To Peel, though, this was subversive stuff.

Repression was no answer. This he knew.
Peel was one of the imaginative few
Who understood that it was wiser to woo
Than to oppose. So what did the PM do?
He began with the clergy. Their influence,
In Ireland, was of major significance.
Lord de Grey took the view that "every priest
"Is a drill sergeant". The truth of this, at least,
Peel recognised – if they were driven to it.
But Sir Robert saw no earthly benefit
In offending the clergy. Draw them on side!
Any other course was certain suicide.

Peel looked to the future. He had to decide.
The College at Maynooth, in County Kildare –
Fifteen miles from Dublin, you may be aware –
Was the chief training ground for priests in its day.
Some four hundred and forty students, they say,
Were in residence in 1844.   **1844**
Yet Maynooth, for all its importance, was poor –
Pitifully poor. It was William Pitt
(The Younger) oddly enough who founded it,
In eager anticipation, it seems,
Of the Union. It was one of Pitt's dreams
That full Catholic emancipation
Would follow, a blessing to the nation.

He was disappointed. It was not to be.
Yet one of the benefits, it's clear to me,

The Early Victorians

Was the grant to Maynooth of eight thousand pounds
(*Per annum*) – not as generous as it sounds,
Of course, fifty years later. Starved of money,
Peel was afraid (he was not being funny)
That Maynooth was sending out, every year,
"Spiritual firebrands" (this was his fear)
"Prepared for mischief... to convulse the country".
Britain was up the proverbial gum tree
Should this scandal continue. The wit of man
Could never devise (so his argument ran)
A fitter way of producing demagogues –
Taught, as they were, by poorly paid pedagogues –
Malignant, sour and "hostile to the law".

"No Popery!" Sir Robert would declare war
On bigotry. With luck, the Repeal movement
Would be compromised by any improvement
In the British government's grant to Maynooth.
Generosity (this was the honest truth)
And persuasion were the keys to progress.
Kill the Association with kindness!

It all seems so obvious in retrospect,
But British Protestants (what did Peel expect?)
Were hostile. The Prime Minister's Maynooth Bill,
Steered through the Commons with commendable skill,
Increased the annual grant more than threefold,
With a one-off special payment (this was bold),
For 'improvements', of some thirty thousand pounds.
In one of those political turnarounds,
Lord John Russell and the Whigs backed the measure.
Sir Robert's backbenchers voiced their displeasure
By voting heavily against. They loathed Peel.

Yet he forged on with his customary zeal,
Supported by the radicals and the Whigs.
Party unity? He didn't care two figs!

Peel was a reformer, less of a Tory
Than a Whig. It had been another story,
Fifteen years before, with the Great Reform Bill.
Peel had been firmly opposed. For good or ill,
Sir Robert was never loth to change his mind –
As he would over corn, I think you will find.

So the Maynooth Bill finally became law.   **1845**
Protestant prejudice I deeply deplore,
As indeed (comforting to note) did the Queen.
Her heart bled for Ireland. I had not foreseen,
I confess, her support for the Catholics.
"Poor Peel ought to be *blessed*" (note the italics)
For the "manly and noble way" he behaved.
The Protestants were little short of depraved.
Peel, she wrote, "stands forth to protect and do good
"To poor Ireland" – as a true Prime Minister should.

Foreign affairs and Lord Palmerston

What of foreign affairs? Lord Aberdeen,
To the evident relief of the Queen,
Had succeeded her *bête noir*, Palmerston,
As Foreign Secretary. Anyone –
And this was a fact that was widely known –
Would have pleased her better than 'Pumicestone',
As Albert and Victoria dubbed him.
A maverick, he would act on a whim –
Ebullient, blunt, undiplomatic
And belligerent. He was pragmatic,
For sure. "We have no eternal allies,"
He said (which occasioned some surprise),
"Nor no perpetual enemies." Well,
That ruffled a few feathers, truth to tell.
Great Britain's interests, in a nutshell,
Were paramount. Others could go to hell.

The Early Victorians

He'd fire off despatches, fit to burst,
Without consulting her Majesty first,
A course that was highly unusual,
If not downright unconstitutional.

Palmerston was also in the habit
Of treating his colleagues in Cabinet
With contempt. He rarely deigned to consult.
Unpopularity was the result,
Not least with other ministers, the Queen,
And Albert. 'Pumicestone', ever serene,
Ploughed on regardless. He had to take charge.

This delighted the populace at large.
Who cared if European heads of state
Deplored his tendency to aggravate?

When Melbourne's government finally fell,
The collapse sounded Palmerston's death knell
As Foreign Secretary. Or did it?
If 'Pam' was disappointed, he hid it.
He was sure to be back and so it proved.
I can't say the royal couple approved,
But following Peel's later fall from grace,
The doughty Palmerston resumed his place.
'Pumicestone' was a stayer. Later still,
Amazingly, believe this if you will,
He himself achieved the exalted rank
Of Prime Minister. If I'm to be frank,
A great part of Palmerston was bluster.
As PM the old man just passed muster.

This we shall see. He was eighty years old –
Two days shy of his eighty-first, we're told –
When he died, still in harness. A great man?
I'm with the Queen. I was never a fan.

Lord Aberdeen

Back to Lord Aberdeen. All said and done,
They were chalk and cheese, he and Palmerston.
Where 'Pam' was impatient, abrasive
And brutal, Aberdeen was persuasive,
Cool and discreet – the perfect diplomat.

Peel was fortunate, no doubt about that,
In his choice of Foreign Secretary.
His experience was legendary.
For Aberdeen had played a vital part,
Three decades earlier (a stunning start),
As the allies closed in on Bonaparte –
As British envoy in 1813
To the Emperor of Austria. Keen,
Astute and barely twenty-nine years old,
Young Aberdeen repaid one hundredfold
The trust vested in him. His leading task –
One of immense importance, since you ask –
Was to attend to British interests
Amid one of the most bitter contests
In Europe's sad and bloody history.

Why he loathed war is no great mystery.
He had witnessed the terrible slaughter
("Wounded men," he wrote, "crying for water,
"Unable to crawl") in 1814,
At Leipzig, a battle foul and obscene.

All the same, Aberdeen's stellar career
In foreign affairs was eclipsed, I fear,
By Palmerston's. Yet 1834
Saw him serve as Secretary for War,
Again for Sir Robert. He knew the score.
So when Peel resumed the premiership,
No captain would steer a steadier ship

Than Aberdeen. Peel's free-trade policy
Cried out for a Foreign Secretary
Who understood that peace and diplomacy
Were key to fostering healthy relations,
In trade and commerce, between wealthy nations.

Aberdeen's character and achievements

He was thorough and cautious, that's my view.
The north-east border, as most people knew,
Between Canada and the state of Maine
Was the source of considerable strain
Between Britain and the United States.

First among Aberdeen's outstanding traits
Was his capacity to compromise.
The disputed terrain was no great prize,
Rocky and barren. It is no surprise

Rhyming History

That Aberdeen, claiming five-twelfths of it,
Ceded the rest. Palmerston had a fit.
An outrage! A sell-out! For Aberdeen,
This modest, early success set the scene
For a wider triumph. For further west,
The States and Britain faced a sterner test.

The 49th parallel had been set
To mark where the States and Canada met,
Though whether in stone was anyone's bet.
For where the common border mattered most –
Namely, approaching the Pacific coast –
The relevant treaty had been unclear.
A literal reading, it would appear,
Deprived Britain of Vancouver Island,
In Canada; also, I understand,
Access to the Columbia River.
President Polk was all of a-quiver.
His slogan, "Fifty-Four Forty or Fight"
Would have meant (to his supporters' delight)
A massive shift of the US border
North of Vancouver. Well out of order.

Peel and Aberdeen both played a blinder.
Neither man needed any reminder
Of the dire consequences of war.
What, after all, was diplomacy for?
Yet neither was a pushover. To Peel,
The prospect of hostilities was real.

Both men stood firm. A compromise was reached.
The 49th parallel would be breached
By way, as it were, of a little kink,
To the south, to embrace (what do you think?)
The lower part of Vancouver Island.
This involved nothing rash or underhand.

The Early Victorians

To have chopped the bottom off – imagine!
Poor Polk, conceding he could never win,
Backed down. What a ridiculous tiff.
"Fifty-Four Forty or Fight" – as if.

Aberdeen was bent on friendship with France.
This looked highly unlikely at first glance.
In the bad old days under Palmerston,
Irreparable damage had been done
After Mehemet Ali (of Egypt)
Invaded Syria. Ali was whipped
Within an inch of his life, sent packing
By Britain and her allies. French backing,
For Ali, though, caused something of a chill.
Humiliation, a bitter pill,
Led to a cooling off of relations
Between Britain and France, both proud nations.

After the Whig defeat of '41,
And with it the exit of Palmerston,
All Europe was overwhelmed with relief,
France in particular. It's my belief
That King Louis Philippe and his PM,
Guizot, preferred, rather than 'us' and 'them',
A true friendship with Britain. Aberdeen,
Ever the peacemaker, was also keen.
So, I am happy to say, was the Queen.
Victoria's uncle, King Leopold,
Had welcomed into the Saxe-Coburg fold
The French King's daughter – by marrying her.
Their difference in age provoked a stir,
But who cared? This was a new beginning.

The French King, more sinned against than sinning,
Sent Victoria an invitation
To visit France. It caused a sensation!

The Queen visits France

For this was the very first time, we're told,
Since the famous Field of the Cloth of Gold –
Where Henry the Eighth met with the French King,
In 1520, for feasting and jousting –
That an English monarch had been entertained
On French terrain. The pleasure was unrestrained.

Louis Philippe had ordered (what a wheeze)
Large quantities of bottled beer and cheese.
He was clearly leaving nothing to chance,
Though, to my mind, importing cheese to France
Was taking coals to Newcastle. The Queen
Enjoyed herself thoroughly. Aberdeen
Regarded the visit as beyond praise.
Indeed, he coined a rather famous phrase:

'Entente cordiale'. The following year –
Perhaps he was missing the bottled beer –
The French King visited Windsor. Peel's fear,
His private concern, was this: could it last?
Were diplomacy's wheels turning too fast?

Relations with the French

For Britain and France were old enemies.
The cessation of hostilities
After the long Napoleonic wars
Was still a living memory. A pause?
A breathing space merely? Heaven forfend!
Sir Robert would fight to the bitter end
For peace and go to almost any length
To avoid conflict. Yet he knew that strength,
Armed strength, was the only sure guarantee
Of keeping Britain prosperous and free.

In the summer of 1843,
A rumpus blew up over Tahiti.
The French invaded! The Tahitian Queen
(Pomare by name), having vented her spleen,
Had little choice but to bow to events.
British protection made better sense,
And this she had sought under Palmerston.
It was refused, but the Brits muddled on.
A certain George Pritchard she appointed
British Consul, hardly the 'Lord's anointed',
But nonetheless a representative
The Tahitians could trust. Well, as I live,
Queen Pomare was forced to accept the French.
To part with the Consul was quite a wrench.
The final straw: Pritchard was arrested.

Peel was livid. He was sorely tested.
Did they reckon he was interested

Rhyming History

In excuses and blandishments? Not he!
Nor was Monsieur Guizot, fortunately,
For the French. The Island of Tahiti
Had been annexed without authority.
The perpetrator, Dupetit-Thouras,
A madcap Admiral, had gone too far.
Peel and Guizot laboured behind the scenes –
Though much of the credit was Aberdeen's –
To defuse the crisis. It caused a scare.
Louis Philippe regretted the affair,
Wishing Tahiti "*au fond de la mer*".

The French press whipped up something of a storm,
Wild and jingoistic, sadly the norm.
The row subsided. The show of goodwill
On the part of both governments, the skill
Of their foreign ministers and the tact
Of the French King triumphed, and that's a fact.
France offered Pritchard compensation.
This was paid not by the French nation,
But out of Louis Philippe's own pocket.
A crisis can take off like a rocket.
It takes wisdom and courage to stop it.

Sad to say, Tahiti was deserted
By the British. True, war was averted
Between Britain and France, but the blunt truth
Is that the French muscled their way back. Strewth.
A bloody conflict between Tahiti
And France ended, alas, in victory
For the French, a blot on our history.
Poor Queen Pomare was humiliated.
Should the British have capitulated
So readily? It was complicated,
True, but so long as Peel could wriggle free,
That was all that bothered him. Shamefully,
Britain cared not a fig for Tahiti.

The Early Victorians

The Spanish succession

That old chestnut, the Spanish succession,
Calculated to bring gloom, depression
And grief to ministers in Britain, Spain,
France and all Europe, had popped up again.
The crowns of France and Spain, all were agreed,
Were never to be joined. Few felt the need
To revisit the Treaty of Utrecht,
Under which French hopes, for ever, were wrecked
With respect to claims to the Spanish throne.
This principle, time-honoured and well known,
Was re-affirmed in 1834.

Young Queen Isabella of Spain, therefore,
Could never marry a French prince. So far,
So good. But there was no absolute bar
On her younger sister, at least in law,
So marrying. By means of this 'back door',
Louis Philippe sought to marry his son
To the *Infanta*. Now, there was no one
Who was fooled about what he was doing.
While his offspring was billing and cooing
With Queen Isabella's little sister –
Sweet as a rosebud, few could resist her –
It was clear that the Queen of Spain herself,
Sickly and weak, could end up on the shelf.
Alternatively, a plan was in place
To marry the Queen (a perfect disgrace)
To one of her Bourbon cousins, alas,
Alleged to be impotent: cruel, crass
And revolting, given that the poor Queen,
Heaven be blessed, was still only thirteen.

The French must have reckoned Peel pretty green
If ever they thought he would swallow that.
Sir Robert was wary. He smelt a rat.

Rhyming History

Aberdeen rode again to the rescue.
A second visit, to the Château d'Eu,
Was arranged for the Queen and Prince Albert.
The whole of Europe was on full alert.

As if by magic the problem was solved.
The French King and Victoria resolved,
By way of a private understanding,
That a match between the son of the King
And the *Infanta* should never take place
Until her sister enjoyed the embrace
Of a husband (neither French nor Coburg)
And had produced (this was getting absurd)
At least two healthy children! Mark my word,
This was a strange brand of diplomacy.
If in doubt, keep it in the family.

Now, Louis Philippe could blow hot and cold.
Indeed, following Peel's fall, we are told,
The French King went back on his word. For now,
However, Aberdeen should take a bow.
Relations between Britain and France
Were sound and amicable. War? No chance.

Rearmament

Sir Robert, for his part, was not so sure.
If you wish for peace, then prepare for war.
The Duke of Wellington, in '44,
Issued stern warnings regarding the state
Of Britain's defences. Rather than wait,
The PM committed the government
To a policy of rearmament,
Costing one million pounds. Aberdeen
Was firmly opposed. From all that he'd seen,
Guizot and the French King were men of peace.
Yet defence spending was on the increase

In France. Wellington was surely not wrong.
The French army, 400,000 strong,
Was a present and overwhelming threat.
Britain's Navy was at her weakest yet:
Nine ships of the line were in commission,
A mere nine – a dangerous omission.

Aberdeen tendered his resignation.
Peel refused to accept it. The nation
Was in need of his cool head, his reserve
And, to give him all due credit, his nerve.
A compromise was reached. Aberdeen stayed.
Peel remained cautious, though less dismayed
Than Wellington, the Commander-in-Chief.
He was seventy-five, beyond belief,
But still a highly respected figure.
Tall and upstanding, he displayed vigour,
Military wisdom and common sense.
The Duke's was the voice of experience.
You ignored him at your peril. Peel knew
When to listen, not talk – Aberdeen too.

Trouble in Afghanistan

Further afield another crisis loomed –
In Afghanistan. The British were doomed.
The old Whig government had authorised
An invasion, and few were surprised
When Palmerston's plan went horribly wrong.
The case in favour had never been strong.
Peel called the project "absurd and insane",
A dispiriting instance, yet again,
Of "Palmerstonian adventurism".
Now, through the cruel, punishing prism
Of government responsibility,
Peel saw the folly of this policy.

Kabul, the Afghan capital city,
Had suffered a bloody atrocity,
Murder most foul. Along with their horses,
6,000 native and British forces
Were put to the sword. The Whigs were to blame,
But for all his errors, Palmerston's name
Remained untarnished. For Peel the crunch came
When the discomforting tidings arrived
That one hundred hostages had survived,
Among them sixteen Englishwomen. Well,
A further twist in the tale, sad to tell,
Was that a new Governor General
For India had just been appointed.

Lord Ellenborough's errors

Sir Robert was deeply disappointed
In Lord Ellenborough, his appointee.
His Lordship was vainglorious, haughty

The Early Victorians

And arrogant. Tread with care, Peel advised.
He feared a bloodbath and I'm not surprised.
Nonetheless, to set the hostages free
Was his overriding priority.

Ellenborough took the opposite course.
Without the faintest display of remorse,
He ordered an immediate retreat
From Afghanistan. His shame was complete –
Or would have been, had not Generals Nott
And Pollock intervened to stop the rot.
While Ellenborough prevaricated,
Nott took a risk, finely calculated.
He stormed north through Kabul (no coward he)
And set the terrified prisoners free.

His Lordship hailed this as his victory!
He raised a few eyebrows, take it from me.
Then he invaded the province of Sind,
In the north-west. Nothing if not thick-skinned!
This was his downfall. Well, it's an ill wind…
The bloody task of annexation,
A dark blot on our reputation,
He entrusted to Sir Charles Napier.

Sir Charles was as sharp as a rapier
And carried out his commission well.
For Napier himself, in a nutshell,
Had no scruples. In his journal he wrote:
"We have no right to seize Sind" (here I quote)
"But we shall do so" (may God have pity)
"And a useful piece of rascality
"It will be." No morals at all, you see.

In a cartoon of the time, "*Peccavi*,"
Napier was seen to cry: "I have sinned" –
A pun. Heaven help the people of Sind.

Rhyming History

Lord Ellenborough's star was fading fast.
His stock was in free fall. He could not last.
At his random exploits Peel was aghast
And was more than happy for heads to roll.
When, in the event, the Board of Control
Moved to dismiss him, Peel was quite content.
The wretch should go, so Ellenborough went.

He had more grandiose plans: Punjab, Kashmir,
Victoria as Empress of India –
Adopted later by Disraeli, I fear.
India he perceived, believe it or not,
As the gateway to Egypt. What utter rot.

Sir Henry Hardinge

Once Ellenborough was out of the way,
Sir Robert could see the clear light of day.
The new Governor General, Hardinge,
Considered the role rather unnerving,
Given the fate of his predecessor.
Nonetheless, Ellenborough's successor
Was pleased to receive this letter from Peel.

Sir Henry Hardinge's mission was to heal.
"If you can keep the peace," good Sir Robert wrote,
"Reduce expense, extend commerce" (again, I quote)
"And strengthen our hold on India by confidence
"In our justice, kindness and wisdom" (thorough good sense),
"You will be received on your return with a welcome
"Infinitely more cordial" (for a job well done)
"Than if you have a dozen victories of which to boast
"And annex the Punjab." In other words, what mattered most
Was a clear sense of responsibility,
Rather than profit and personal glory.
A vain hope, alas, but that's another story.

The Early Victorians

Pressures of office: budgets, tax and tariffs

Back to domestic politics. Old Peel,
Fifty-six years of age, had nerves of steel.
Yet the strains of office were sure to tell.
Sir Robert felt increasingly unwell,
Complaining of "tiredness in the head,"
The cause of which, it is commonly said,
Was a shooting accident years before.
For this there was neither comfort nor cure.
The wretched symptoms resembled, I fear,
The "noise of boiling water" in his ear.
Peel was overworked, as simple as that.
Yet in spite of the ear, and feeling flat,
He persevered. There were tough times ahead.
1845 was a watershed.

First, the budget. Despite sustained attacks,
He resolved to renew the income tax.
The surplus this was expected to yield
Was to benefit not just the well-heeled,
But ordinary people across the land.
For Sir Robert was quick to understand
That cutting tariffs further was the key
To sustaining a strong economy,
Not for the few, but for everybody.

His critics professed themselves astonished,
As tariffs were completely abolished
On well over half those commodities
Still subject to irksome import duties.
These included raw cotton. Cuts like these
Gave a huge boost to those new industries
Which needed such items from overseas.
Great Britain sadly had been on her knees
When Sir Robert took the reins. Five years on,
The country was booming. Peel's halo shone!

Rhyming History

Folk were healthier and better nourished,
Men were richer and families flourished.
With the deficit a threat no longer,
Peel could relax. Even the Church was stronger.
He allowed himself a rare pat on the back,
Yet within a year he was facing the sack.

'45 was a very wet summer.
For farmers, of course, this was a bummer,
But for ministers it was far, far worse.
A terrible harvest gave cause to curse.
High food prices threatened civil unrest.
Peel was nervous, he readily confessed.

The Irish potato famine

Poor harvests were one thing, potato blight
Another altogether. Ireland's plight
Was critical. Would the rain never stop?
One third of the country's potato crop
Turned bad. The fungus that rotted the spud
Had a thirst for damp and it loved the mud.
The following year, at enormous cost,
Three-quarters of the Irish crop was lost.

Potatoes were the staple peasant food.
Some three million (that's a multitude)
Ate nothing else, and I do mean nothing.
Most adult males (now this is sobering)
Ate between twelve and fourteen pounds a day.
Imagine then the scale of the dismay
When the potato crop failed. Poor Ireland.
Thousands perished as famine stalked the land.
Peel was well aware of the need to act.
In secret, and with some degree of tact,
He drew up plans for the import of maize
From America. These were early days.

The Early Victorians

Was one hundred thousand pounds' worth enough?
Well hardly, but this was alien stuff.
Peasants never got used to baking bread.
They preferred the potato. Enough said.

However, as the deadly fungus spread,
Maize became more popular bit by bit.
Government advice on how to cook it
Increased the demand. What of the market?
Forget *laissez-faire*, at least for a while.
The peasants were starving. It took some guile
On Peel's part, with his belief in free trade,
To 'fix' the market. But the case was made.
He pressed on regardless and unafraid.

Thank God for Sir Robert's humanity.
His successor, I can tell you for free,
Lord John Russell, tried another angle,
Landing himself in a rare old tangle.
Be that as it may. We must take a pause
And turn again to the dreaded Corn Laws.

Rhyming History

The Corn Laws

The two subjects were closely related.
Peel must certainly have calculated
That to import foreign maize duty-free –
To cope with the Irish emergency –
Would undermine his present policy
On the Corn Laws. Whether temporary
Or not, to waive the tariffs in Ireland
And nowhere else would appear underhand,
Prejudicial and inconsistent.
Repeal had to come. Peel was insistent.
The Tories to a man were resistant.
He cared not a jot. The Corn Laws must go.

The Irish famine cast a long shadow,
But gave Peel the perfect excuse to do
What he knew in his heart he needed to.
There was simply no choice. Trade tariffs stank,
So tariffs went and we have Peel to thank.
The PM proposed the total repeal
"Absolute and for ever" (was this for real?)
"Of all duties" (these the very words of Peel)
"On all articles of subsistence". Something,
He knew, had to give. It was all or nothing.

The Tory party split

Yet the logic of his position
Came up against stiff opposition
In Cabinet. The party would be "broken".
It was the bluff Lord Stanley who had spoken,
Secretary for War and the Colonies.
His Lordship, understandably ill at ease,
Resigned from the government. The party split.
The Tories suffered a political fit
And would be out of office for thirty years.

The Early Victorians

Sir Robert resigns

The PM was less concerned, it appears,
With party unity than were his peers.
He failed to carry his colleagues with him.
Too bad! So he resigned – not on a whim,
But on principle. Good Lord Aberdeen
Supported him, as indeed did the Queen.
She and Prince Albert were both horrified
At their loss. Sir Robert they deified.

Nevertheless, it was time to decide.
Who should the Queen now send for? Peel advised
Lord John Russell. She was hardly surprised.
The leader of the Whigs, of Reform Bill fame,
He had urged repeal. The Tories were to blame
For hanging on to a rotten old law
That they should have abandoned years before.

Peel was happy to make it crystal clear
That Russell had his support. Never fear,
If the Whigs could steer a new Corn Bill through,
He stood behind them. What else could he do?

Poor Lord John made a hopeless fist of it.
Lord Palmerston (this was the gist of it)
Was tipped again for the Foreign Office –
Highly unpopular with the Queen this,
But she was powerless to intervene.
Within days, to the relief of the Queen,
Russell was obliged to tell her Majesty
That he had failed (a personal tragedy)
In his efforts to form a government.
Old 'Pam' would have been in his element
Back in the Foreign Office, but Lord Grey
Greeted the proposal with deep dismay.

Grey (son of the former Prime Minister)
Considered the appointment sinister,
Fraught with danger and far from sensible.
To Russell they were indispensable,
Grey and Palmerston. Both dug their heels in.
Neither man would budge, so neither could win.

Peel back in office

So Victoria sent for Peel again!
Lord John's failure was Sir Robert's gain.

For this was the critical watershed
In his career. Forget pains in the head,
Forget exhaustion. He told the Queen
That the current crisis, though unforeseen,
Afforded him the opportunity
To sacrifice all to her Majesty –
All, that is, save his honour. A Corn Bill
He would therefore present, for good or ill,
To Parliament. Take it or leave it.
That was their choice, they'd better believe it.

So Peel agreed to form a government.
He asked for neither counsel nor consent
From his Cabinet. Most now stood by him.
Acutely aware the prospects were grim,
They were strong in their service to the Queen.
As firm and true as he had ever been,
The Duke of Wellington, deaf as a post
And seventy-six, knew what mattered most
Was loyalty to Queen Victoria.
With a new-found sense of euphoria,
Peel carried his reluctant Cabinet.
Like a man restored to life, fighting fit,
He relished a challenge and this was it.

In January, 1846,   **1846**
He faced the Commons. There was no quick fix.
The Tories were vehemently opposed
(His own party) to the measures proposed.
They sat on their hands (appallingly rude)
As Peel, their leader, in defiant mood,
Invoked the "high honour" of his office
And expressed himself determined (mark this)
"To hold it by no servile tenure". Well,
His speech sounded many an alarm bell
Among the Tory protectionists –
Dyed-in-the-wool agriculturalists,
The 'landed interest'. The benefits
They enjoyed through tariffs fed their profits.
They supported the Laws, and here is why:
The duty on corn kept the prices high.

Sir Robert given a rough ride

Benjamin Disraeli put the boot in.
If ever he spotted a mortal sin,
It was putting country before party.
Disraeli was a bit of a smarty.
Fancied as one of the '*literati*'
(He wrote novels), it seemed his favoured role
Was working his way up the greasy pole.
Fiercely ambitious, he taunted Peel.
With an unbecoming and misplaced zeal,
He accused him of "petty larceny"
And being a "burglar" (pretty ghastly)
"Of other intellects" on a grand scale.

He goaded Sir Robert without avail,
But remained a lethal thorn in his side,
Smooth and contemptuous, subtle and snide.
Should Peel have been given an easy ride
Or made to fight for his life? You decide.

Disraeli did not make all the running.
Peel's command of the Commons was stunning.
Britain should not shrink from competition.
This was the crux. Sir Robert's position
Was clear. The country could "advance" or "recede".
Free trade was the only sure way to proceed.

What of the vote? Well, the government won,
But the Tory party was quite undone.
Tories against: two hundred and thirty-one;
Tories for: one hundred and twelve, just one third
Of the party vote. Now it may sound absurd,
But Peel was not too bothered. Upon my word,
He never expected to do much better.
Lord John Russell's Whigs performed to the letter:
Two hundred and twenty-seven voted for,
A mere eleven against. A win, therefore:

The Early Victorians

A majority of ninety-seven.
On the Bill's second reading, great Heaven,
This majority was slightly reduced,
Down to eighty-eight. The fuss this produced
Was trivial. On the 16th of May
(Third reading) the Bill, I'm happy to say,
Was approved by ninety-eight votes. Hooray!

The debates took their toll. Peel was abused,
Heckled and jeered. The poor chap stood accused
Of treachery, disloyalty… and theft.
Had the man no shame or dignity left,
Asked Disraeli? "Let men stand, right or wrong,
"On their principles" (Dizzy was on song);
Reward them not for "alteration"
Or "political tergiversation".

Long words! But Peel gave as good as he got.
He hit back at Benjamin like a shot.
If the Hon. Member despised him so much,
Why had he "solicited" (a deft touch)
Office from Peel a mere five years before?
The PM, pushing at an open door,
Might easily have brought Disraeli down,
Denounced him as a liar and a clown.
For Ben denied the letter existed.

Now, had the Prime Minister persisted,
And produced it, Dizzy would have been toast.
Surely what mattered to Sir Robert most
Was the Corn Bill. He did not want to crow.
Such a letter did exist, this we know,
But Peel preferred not to put it on show.
Why should a fellow choose to stoop so low?

Next stop, the Lords. Nobody appeared keen
To lead for the government. That 'has-been',

113

Lord Ripon (the former Lord Goderich,
Tearful, confused and a bit of a snitch),
Accepted the challenge, then changed his mind.
Ripon, alas (without being unkind),
Was a washout. Step forward Wellington!
Here was a man who could get a job done.
The only hitch was that he disagreed
With the policy! But Tories take heed:
The Iron Duke was there to serve the Queen,
As true a subject as had ever been.

He set about the business with a will.
He warned that should the Lords throw out the Bill
The future of the House would be in doubt.
Friend and foe were agreed: the Duke had clout.

Repeal of the Corn Laws

In blissful ignorance of the Corn Laws,
He championed the House of Commons' cause.
The lower House, after frenzied debate,
Had approved the Bill. The government's fate
Should never depend on their Lordships' whim.
He stood firm on the Bill, and good for him.
Lord John Russell's Whigs were whipped into line.
The Bill was passed (an encouraging sign)
By a respectable majority,
On second reading, of nearly fifty.
On June the 25th the Bill was passed.
The pesky Corn Laws were repealed at last.

Continual hounding of Sir Robert

Disraeli, though, was still on the warpath.
Would he throw in the sponge? Don't make me laugh.
If he couldn't kill the Bill, his intent
Was now to finish off the government.

The Early Victorians

They say revenge is a dish best served cold.
Peel's opponents were determined and bold –
Bitter, disappointed and sore to boot.
Disraeli would strike at the very root,
Viz. Peel himself. His allies followed suit.

Their target was the so-called Irish Bill.
The famine in Ireland, an issue still,
Had steadily given rise over time
To a hike in theft and violent crime.
The Irish Bill sought stiffer penalties
For breaches of the peace. Peel's enemies
United against this modest measure.

Disraeli took a sadistic pleasure
In pushing him to the limit. The Whigs,
The Corn Laws apart, didn't care two figs
For Peel. In a rare show of unity,
They seized this golden opportunity
To team up with Dizzy's dismal cohorts
And inflict a defeat. That worst of sports,
Lord Bentinck, son of the former PM,
Lord Portland, was prominent amongst them –
Disraeli's pals, that is. It was Bentinck,
Rather than he, who drove Peel to the brink.

Bentinck charged him with hounding George Canning
To his death years before. This was shocking,
And caused more than a minor sensation.

Bentinck had a dodgy reputation.
It was Catholic emancipation
That lay at the heart of his charge. Young Peel
(As he then was) never sought to conceal
His doubts regarding Canning's policy.
He'd professed himself, in all honesty,

Rhyming History

Against emancipation. It took nerve,
But when offered a post he declined to serve.
Only later did he come to change his mind.
No hypocrite he, it was crass and unkind
To pretend, as Bentinck now did, that Peel
Had misled Canning. Yet the charge was real.
Canning died in office, the shortest term
In history, as records will confirm.
To think of blaming Peel was a disgrace,
Political poison, shameful and base.

The spite with which Bentinck launched his attack
Was awful. Peel was so taken aback
That he determined to challenge Bentinck
To a duel. He was urged to rethink,
But it shows how tempers were running high.

Disraeli's treachery is hard to deny.
His behaviour was reprehensible.
The Irish Bill was temperate, sensible
And well considered. The Whigs were opposed,
And in normal times one might have supposed
That the Tories would have stood, to a man,
Behind Peel. But Disraeli's malign plan
Was to force the government to its knees.

In concert with the Whigs, Irish MPs
And assorted protectionist Tories,
He ensured that the Bill was thrown out.
The defeat was a veritable rout,
A majority of seventy-three
Against the measure. Yet take it from me,
Peel was relaxed. Do you want to know why?
His disappointment was hard to deny,
But tidings of a far sweeter victory
Reached him that morning and these made history.

The Early Victorians

For it was on the 26th of June,
At one a.m. (not a moment too soon),
That news came through that the Lords had approved
The Corn Bill. Small wonder that Peel was moved.
Sad as he was to lose the Irish Bill,
His greater work was done. It was God's will.

Peel resigns

Victoria's discomfort was complete.
"In one breath," she wrote, "triumph and defeat."
She referred to "that dreadful Disraeli".
It seems extraordinary to me
That, oozing honeyed words and flattery,
Dizzy would become the Queen's favourite.
For he it was who coaxed her, bit by bit,
Out of her widow's seclusion. Well,
How he managed that challenge, time will tell.

For now, Peel travelled to the Isle of Wight,
To Osborne House (Victoria's delight,
Her summer home), to tender to the Queen
His resignation. It was some scene:
Her Majesty was a little tearful,
Peel, we are told, remarkably cheerful.
Chatty (for once) and far from downhearted,
He told his sovereign, as they parted,
That suddenly being out of office
Was like a dream. The Queen's response to this?
"A *very bad* dream." Note her italics.

Sir Robert was finished with politics.
On the Monday of the following week,
A hushed House of Commons heard him speak.
Peel announced his resignation,
Content to let his reputation

Rhyming History

Rest with those whose lot it was to labour
And "earn their daily bread" (words to savour)
"By the sweat of their brow, when they shall recruit
"Their exhausted strength" (the speech was a beaut)
"With abundant and untaxed food". Injustice
He deplored. If anything drove him, it was this.

He left the House of Commons by a side door.
Within minutes the large crowd was on a roar.

Their hero they had instantly recognised.
The cheering continued (I'm hardly surprised)
Long after he had reached his house: simple folk,
Who owed their very lives, no word of a joke,
To Sir Robert Peel. He had a letter from one fan,
From Nottingham, thanking him (this is how it began)
For "unfettering the staff of life to the poor man".

The Early Victorians

Enter Lord John Russell

Victoria again summoned Russell,
Her only choice, as far as she could tell.
Leader of the Whigs since Lord Melbourne's fall,
Lord John was hardly to her taste at all.
Volatile, radical, vain and flaky,
His grasp of economics was shaky,
His relations with his colleagues poor
And his zeal for reform hard to ignore.

Lord John Russell's principal claim to fame
Was the Great Reform Act. This made his name.
He helped draft the Bill and was its pilot
Through the Commons. He ran the full gamut
Of hostility and opposition,
But held fast to his long-held position
As a reformer. Folk were overawed.
At forty years old he reaped his reward,
With swift promotion to the Cabinet.
A rosy future was a pretty safe bet.
Earl Grey's successor, Melbourne, in '34,
Made him Leader of the House. Need I say more?

In Melbourne's next ministry (from '35
To '41) he displayed wisdom, drive,
Passion and imagination.
A champion of education,
He provided a firm foundation
For Gladstone's later Education Act.

As Home Secretary, Lord John's impact
Was lasting and humane. He introduced
A raft of penal reforms. He reduced,
To his great credit, the number of crimes
Punishable by death. These were hard times,

But (to cite just one example) forgery
No longer attracted the death penalty.
He built on Peel's reforms. On the Isle of Wight,
At Parkhurst, with considerable foresight,
He established a prison for juveniles.
In this he was ahead of his peers by miles.
He also introduced an inspectorate
Of prisons – a reform of lasting merit.

So all boded well, on the face of it.
When Peel resigned, would we see a new Pitt?

Lord John's failure

Sadly not. For Russell was a washout.
His six years as PM, without a doubt,
Were an abject failure. He lacked clout,
Presiding over a weak ministry
With no sense of purpose or strategy.
He was shambolic and disorganised.
Many a correspondent was surprised
To receive post meant for others (the dope)
Addressed, but sent in the wrong envelope!

It could not have been easy being small.
Lord John was just five feet, five inches tall.
This should not, of course, have mattered at all,
But topping the scales at eight stone in weight,
The nickname 'little Johnny' was his fate.
'Finality Jack' they also called him,
After he had pledged himself, on a whim,
Against further reform of the franchise.
This was in '35, and far from wise.
To offer such a hostage to fortune
Was sheer lunacy. He soon changed his tune,
Campaigning strongly throughout his career
For more reform – a long struggle, I fear.

The Early Victorians

Lord John Russell was the first man, we hear,
To enjoy a hot bath every day –
The very first Englishman, anyway.

Remember Queen Elizabeth the First,
To whom the mere thought of bathing was cursed,
Alleged to have taken two baths a year
"Whether she needed one or not". Oh, dear.

The continuing famine in Ireland

Little Johnny's first challenge was Ireland,
And it nearly drove him into the sand.
The potato famine was at its height
When he took office. The terrible blight
Had been dreadful enough in '45.
The poorest peasants struggled to survive.

Rhyming History

Many thousands sadly lost the battle.
Potatoes were their livelihood. Cattle,
Fish, corn, game – these were means of sustenance
Alien to the poor. It was nonsense,
Not far short of criminal, to argue,
As Sir Charles Wood was not ashamed to do
(Lord John Russell's Chancellor) in full flow:
"Where the people refuse to work or sow
"They must starve." Sir Charles had no more money.

The Chancellor was not being funny,
But mark this. A small measure of relief,
A mere seven million pounds, good grief,
Was thrown at the problem. Ten times more
Was found to finance the Crimean War,
Less than a decade later. *Laissez-faire*
Was the watchword. As I'm sure you're aware,
The free market was gospel. Government
Distanced itself from the predicament
Of the hungry and starving. Funds were cut
To the relief committees. That tough nut,
Sir Charles, iron-hearted, blinkered and mean,
Dug in his heels, refused to intervene
And pursued to the death (literally)
Liberal economics. Cheerfully,
Meanwhile, large consignments of Irish wheat,
To make John Russell's discomfort complete,
Were harvested and shipped from Irish ports.
Small wonder the peasants were out of sorts.

Up to five-sixths of the potato crop
Was lost in '46. Caught on the hop,
The new Whig ministry sat on its hands.
The worsening crisis, one understands,
Hardened its attitude against relief.
Food depots were closed down (beyond belief),

The Early Victorians

Maize imports (Peel's policy) suspended,
And all government subsidy ended.
True, the Irish Poor Law was extended
To 'outdoor relief', but this depended
On local efforts which, in a nutshell,
Were inadequate at best. Sad to tell,
Landlords showed little mercy. Some, it's true,
Were charitable chaps, but they were few.

Others took advantage of the famine
To harass their tenants. It was no sin
To drive the wretches out. Pay up or go!
No quarter. No mercy. Nor were they slow,
These wealthy farmers, to give chase to thieves
Caught stealing from their fields. No one believes,
Even in hindsight, that to prosecute
Hungry families for pilfering fruit,
Veg and berries was anything but mean.
To starve them to death was simply obscene.

Some landlords were mere absentees. Of peers
In the House of Lords many, it appears
(Over twenty *per cent*), owned Irish land.
It's not that difficult to understand
Their deep reluctance to become involved.
Out of sight, out of mind. Problem solved.

Lord Palmerston, Foreign Secretary,
A key player in Russell's ministry
(Though he sat in the Commons*), was one such.
The great famine didn't bother him much.
Owning 10,000 acres in Sligo,
His tenants were the lowest of the low.

---

*Ineligible, I should make it clear,
To sit in the Lords as an Irish peer.

Rhyming History

'Pam' supported government policy
With respect to denying subsidy
To the 'able-bodied'. He showed pity,
However, to a limited extent.
He made a pledge. Palmerston was content
To encourage the emigration,
Among his tenant population,
Of those who sought a better life abroad.
The hungry, the unwashed and the ignored
(*Viz.* the 'surplus' Irish) had their fares paid
To Canada, no less. They had it made.

Irish emigration

By late autumn 1847,   **1847**
2,000 of his tenants, great Heaven,
Had set sail. They were given, on board ship,
Hot rum punch, courtesy of his Lordship.
Sadly, when the liquor went to their head,
He offered coffee and biscuits instead.
He had promised them, upon arrival,
Up to five pounds per head. Their survival
In Quebec, for sure, depended on this.

Their promised life of Canadian bliss
Proved to be a tragic illusion.
Whether a result of confusion,
Backsliding or maladministration,
The Irish created a sensation,
Though regrettably for the wrong reasons.
Most critically, that worst of seasons,
The Canadian winter, was at its height.
The emigrants' sad and desperate plight,
Poor souls, had to be seen to be believed.
A better life? Far from being 'relieved',
They landed famished and bitterly cold,
Women and children, barefoot, young and old,

The Early Victorians

Many in rags, some with no clothes at all.
The truth is calculated to appal:
On one ship alone, dozens of poor folk
Died on the voyage, no word of a joke.
One woman had to be carried ashore,
Naked, in a blanket. Need I say more?
Thousands were left to wander through the snow,
Hungry and helpless, with nowhere to go.

Palmerston was heavily criticised
In Parliament. I am not surprised.
He blamed his agents. He had done his best.
His wretched tenants, needy and distressed,
Wrote letters to the Canadian press –
Illiterate, clearly under duress –
With expressions of deepest gratitude
To their landlord. I've no wish to be rude,
But of sheer arrogance, hypocrisy,
Humbug, cant and brazen mendacity,
Lord Palmerston was the epitome.

Hailed as the greatest statesman of his age,
A colossus bestriding the world stage,
'Pam' is an enigma. His bravado –
He was something of a desperado –
His brinkmanship, swagger and art of bluff,
His making of policy off the cuff,
Unsettled colleagues and angered the Queen.
His private conduct was downright obscene –
One alleged case of an attempted rape,
I kid you not. Yet there is no escape:
Palmerston was an arresting figure,
A man of most astonishing vigour,
Courage and intellectual rigour.
Be that as it may, I was never a fan.
I'm with Victoria. I detest the man.

Russell and Clarendon, no friends of the Irish

Although no accurate record survives,
The catastrophic famine claimed the lives
Of a million victims, maybe more.
As if he'd never thought of it before,
Lord John Russell, the crisis at its height,
Laid claim to the moral high ground. He might,
Just might, open soup kitchens for the poor!
So he did, thus claiming for evermore
That no one on his watch had starved to death.
All lies, of course. He should have saved his breath.

A footnote. The Viceroy, safe in Dublin,
Throughout the course of the cruel famine,
Pigged himself out. Lord Clarendon, the swine,
Spent thirteen hundred pounds a year on wine,
Three hundred on fish and thousands on meat.
I'm glad his Lordship had enough to eat.

The Early Victorians

The whole system was rotten to the core.
To add to the horror, there's one thing more.
While a worker brought home eightpence a day –
With no food to spend it on anyway –
The Viceroy earned (prepare to shed a tear)
A cool twenty thousand smackers a year.

It's time to take a break from politics –
John Russell, *laissez-faire* economics
And the starving Irish: a deadly mix.

The Brontë sisters

1847: a vintage year
For novels. The three finest to appear
Were written by three sisters, the Brontës.
Published initially, by degrees,
Under pseudonyms, it was 'Currer Bell'
Who wrote *Jane Eyre*. I'm delighted to tell
That the novel did exceedingly well,
Quickly becoming the talk of the town.

Queen Victoria couldn't put it down:
"Powerfully and admirably written,
"Such a fine tone in it" (she was smitten),
"Such fine religious feeling." Poor Jane.
A clergyman's daughter, diffident, plain
And small of stature, she was sent to school
To Lowood. The *régime* there was cruel,
Repressive and brutal. Jane was witness
To the death, after a painful illness,
Of a dear schoolfellow in great distress –
A story of misery, loss and grief.

The account of Lowood defies belief.
Yet the school the Brontë girls attended
Was worse by far. Cowan Bridge offended

Rhyming History

All standards of decency, charity,
Godliness and common humanity.
The place was run by one Carus Wilson,
A malign and sadistic clergyman
Of the hell-fire brand. Fortunate indeed,
According to this monster's twisted creed,
Was the child who died in a state of grace,
Trusting only in God – wicked and base.

Luckily, at the tender age of eight,
Charlotte Brontë narrowly missed a date
With Death. Her older sisters' tragic fate
Was to die, under Wilson's dismal care,
Of consumption. Not unlike Jane Eyre,
Charlotte watched her sister Elizabeth,
At eleven, draw her very last breath.
Maria went first to the grave, aged ten.
Thank God that the Reverend Brontë then
(Why only then?) removed little Charlotte
And Emily (barely more than a tot)
From that poisonous institution.

Blessed with a robust constitution,
Sturdier than her sisters anyway,
Young Charlotte lived to fight another day –
As did Jane Eyre. To give the plot away
Would spoil your pleasure. Suffice it to say
That the Queen, who nursed a passion for books,
Sat up late into the night, on tenterhooks,
Reading with Albert. Rochester's crazed wife,
The fire that threatened his very life
And left him blind, with the loss of a hand,
Was "awfully thrilling", we understand.
Jane's character was "a beautiful one".
Victoria's joy though, all said and done –
At the risk of sounding condescending –
Was the novel's "peaceful, happy ending".

The Early Victorians

In the selfsame year it was 'Ellis Bell'
Who wrote *Wuthering Heights*. This sold less well.
Emily's masterpiece, her only book,
Would enjoy in time (and some time it took)
The overwhelming, popular success
That it merited. I have to confess
That the wild moors, the "arid wilderness
"Of furze and whinstone", are not to all tastes.
Cathy and Heathcliff, on the rugged wastes,
Tug at the heartstrings, lovers of passion,
Brooding and dark, in true Gothic fashion.

It is fair to say that *Wuthering Heights*
Is the Brontë novel that most delights.
Ask anyone at random who has read it.
To Emily Brontë's eternal credit,
It's highly likely to be their favourite.

That same year again, amazing but true,
The third sister, Anne ('Acton Bell' to you),
Wrote *Agnes Grey*, a middling success.
Another story of a governess,
This (unlike *Jane Eyre*) is a simple tale,
Conceived on a modest, domestic scale.
Intelligent, sympathetic and strong,
And blessed with a keen sense of right and wrong,
Agnes finds her charges surly and rude.
Her life of unremitting solitude
Is interrupted… Her father falls ill…
She arrives too late… Through sheer force of will,
She opens a school… Then Agnes finds love,
Marrying happily… Heavens above!
Was this Mills and Boon? Far from it, I'd say.

Life for a governess was no holiday.
Paid a pittance and routinely abused,
Her talents scandalously underused,

Rhyming History

Her prospects were bleak, I have to confess.
Anne Brontë was blazing a trail, no less,
For the rights of women. Few, as a rule,
Were daring enough to found their own school.
Agnes combined this with family life,
Finding success as a mother and wife.
That was some achievement in those dark days.
Agnes (and Anne) are worthy of high praise.

Anne's second, *The Tenant of Wildfell Hall*
(Her last work), has the power to enthral.
In this astonishing book, a young wife
Struggles with her bleak and unhappy life
With a debauched husband – Anne in her prime.
This novel too was ahead of its time.
The reviews were mixed. That's probably why.

The younger Brontë sisters were to die
Within six months of each other. Poor Anne,
So rich in talent… Her sickness began
In 1848, the very year
The Tenant of Wildfell Hall would appear.
Her sister Emily's decline, I fear,
Was hastened, in those grim December days,
By Anne's own agony. This will amaze,
But Emily refused all medicine.
Wracked with consumption, she was pencil-thin.
The old carpenter who made her coffin
Had never before built one so narrow
For an adult, as slim as an arrow:
A mere sixteen inches wide, great Heaven,
For a length (her height) of five feet seven.

Emily died shortly before Christmas,
Followed by her beloved Anne, alas,
On the 28th of May, '49.
Charlotte witnessed the terrible decline

The Early Victorians

Of both her loving sisters. She lived on
For six years longer after they were gone.
She wrote *Shirley* ('49) and *Villette*
('53), the latter book her best yet,
According to some. She found happiness
In marriage to the curate, no less,
Of her father's parish. Within a year
Poor Charlotte died (prepare to shed a tear)
From typhoid fever during pregnancy.

Why should this surprise us? Tragically,
Haworth was one of the least sanitary
Villages in Yorkshire. Its water supply
Flowed directly under the graveyard, that's why,
Poisoning every mouthful people drank.
The villagers had typhoid fever to thank
For the fact that half the population
Died before they were six. Inhalation
Of the foul stench from the parsonage graveyard
Was deadly and dangerous. Having regard
To the curse of contaminated water,
It's some miracle that one Brontë daughter
Survived to the ripe old age of thirty-eight.

The future was too morbid to contemplate.
You reserved your slot with the undertaker,
And in Haworth prepared to meet your maker
At twenty-six. This was the average age
Of death. Coffins and headstones were all the rage.

The incomparable Charles Dickens

It's a privilege to celebrate in rhyme
The finest storyteller of all time,
The great Charles Dickens. That's my view, at least.
His novels are a veritable feast

Rhyming History

Of character and eccentricity,
Dark satire and social comedy.
They plumb the depths of vice and villainy,
Violence, murder and depravity,
Then soar to the heights of humanity –
Pity, compassion and charity.
Touched at times with sentimentality,
A blemish I can readily forgive,
The novels have endured, proof positive
That Dickens' plots and his characters *live*.

His secret? He wrote about what he knew.
Young Charles rescued himself, one of the few,
From poverty. When he was ten years old,
His education was put on hold
When his poor father plunged deep into debt,
Committed later, his lowest ebb yet,
To the Marshalsea, a debtors' gaol.
Charles was then twelve. Was he destined to fail?
This he dreaded. He laboured for a year,
In work that afforded him little cheer,
In a blacking factory, near Charing Cross,
Pasting labels on bottles. I'm at a loss.
Six bob a week he earned, day in, day out,
Grim and depressing, no shadow of doubt.

Experience of grinding poverty
He described as "the secret agony
"Of my soul" which "no word can express…
"Utterly neglected and hopeless".
Only Catherine Hogarth, his wife,
Knew the story of his early life –
She and his closest friend, John Forster,
Theatre critic and biographer.

His father's release from the Marshalsea
Won Charles his freedom from the factory.

At fifteen, after a return to school,
He swapped his pupil's desk for a clerk's stool
In a modest solicitor's office,
An opportunity too good to miss.
Characters that hold his readers agog –
Jaggers and Tulkinghorn, Dodson and Fogg,
As well as *Bleak House* (its intricate plot,
Jarndyce v. Jarndyce) – were, as like as not,
Inspired by these early days in the law.

Life as a clerk proved a terrible bore.
In the evenings he studied shorthand
And (still in his teens, you should understand)
He took work as a reporter, freelance,
In Doctors' Commons. Here, by happy chance,
He mastered his craft observing the clerks,
Bailiffs, scriveners and turnkeys. What larks!

Rhyming History

Dip into *Bleak House, Martin Chuzzlewit,*
David Copperfield or *Little Dorrit,*
You'll be sure to find a lawyer in it,
Or a law officer, proud or humble,
Counsel or beadle, Buzfuz or Bumble.

The Pickwick Papers was a famous hit.
Dickens' first, it enjoyed the benefit
Of publication in serial parts,
Monthly instalments. It soon touched the hearts
Of thousands. After the slowest of starts
(A mere four hundred copies) it took off
Like a rocket. At one shilling (don't scoff)
The issue price was a spit and a cough
Against the cost of an average book,
At thirty-two shillings. Do take a look.
The adventures of Samuel Pickwick,
Comic, romantic and mock-heroic,
Proved a phenomenal, instant success.

Up to 40,000 readers, no less,
Were soon enjoying the foibles, mishaps
And scrapes of that charming trio of chaps,
Snodgrass, Tupman and Winkle. Sam Weller,
Cockney servant, an excellent fella,
Made his first appearance in issue four.
Dickens was pushing at an open door.
Sales hit the roof. Cynics who had surmised
That monthly instalments were ill advised
Were silenced, and not a little surprised.
Dickens set a trend. Trollope, Thackeray
And George Eliot would choose the same way,
Published, all, in the journals of the day.
The book is set in the pre-railway age.
Nostalgia colours every page,
A disappearing world: Dingley Dell,
Pre-Reform England, vanishing pell-mell.

The Early Victorians

In spite of its old-fashioned atmosphere,
One thing nonetheless is strikingly clear:
Dickens' unerring sense of comedy –
What one called his "endless fertility
"In laughter-causing detail". Well, that said,
Samuel Pickwick and his friends, well fed,
Affluent, witty and game for a laugh,
Merit little more than a paragraph
In a sweep through the Dickens catalogue.

Some of the books can be rather a slog,
Bleak House being one, *Dombey and Son* too.
But what marked Charles Dickens out, what was new,
Was his unique view of society
In all its infinite variety –
Complex, comic and corrupt. Property
And privilege, greed and pomposity;
Sorrow, disease and grinding poverty –
These were Dickens' canvas. It seems obscene
That Melbourne sought to influence the Queen
To abandon *Oliver Twist*. The poor,
His lordship urged, it was best to ignore!
Her verdict I find rather depressing.
Far from finding the story distressing,
The book, she wrote, was "very interesting".

So Melbourne oversaw the Queen's reading!
For a person of her rank and breeding,
Oliver Twist he found unsuitable.
All his best efforts to be dutiful
Were misconceived. She could never have feared
The Pickwick Papers. The whole book appeared
(Its final instalment) four months after
Victoria's accession: laughter,
Colour, adventure – all much to her taste.
If she missed out on *Pickwick*, what a waste.

Rhyming History

Dickens' first seven novels were published
In as many years. Folk were astonished.
Samuel Pickwick appeared on the scene
In the very same year as England's Queen,
Soon to be followed by *Oliver Twist*.
Nicholas Nickleby, not to be missed,
Was next, a tale of corruption and vice –
Let Mulberry Hawk in his cups suffice –
Coupled with wonderful hilarity
In Vincent Crummles and his family,
His daughter, the 'Infant Phenomenon',
And his *troupe* of actors, glorious fun.

Nickleby is a life-affirming book,
And a tragic one. That dastardly crook,
Ralph Nickleby, uncle to Nicholas,
Exploits his mother and sister, alas.
Ralph is the treacherous father, no less,
Of poor, unfortunate Smike. Fecklessness,
Cruelty and pure unbridled malice,
All are present, I should warn you of this.

Next came *The Old Curiosity Shop.*
The young Charles Dickens was writing non-stop.
Barnaby Rudge was also in his mind,
A less popular book, I think you'll find,
But in my view one of his very best.
The Gordon Riots! He rose to the test:
A brilliant historical story,
Set in 1780, strong, gory
And violent; but still a touching tale
Of young Barnaby, on a human scale.

The Old Curiosity Shop, to me,
Though laced with its fair share of villainy,
Is far and away too soppy by half,
So sentimental that you want to laugh.

The Early Victorians

Not so the Victorians; dear me, no!
For all its diabolic undertow,
The Old Curiosity Shop struck gold.
Some 100,000 copies were sold,
A number without parallel, we're told.

When little Nell lost her struggle for life,
Reports of her passing cut like a knife.
Her death was written up in the broadsheets.
Grown men wept openly in the streets.
Queen Victoria must surely have died,
Thought one American on the quayside
At Southampton. My, how the people cried.

Dickens' sixth novel, *Martin Chuzzlewit*,
Was rather less of a sure-fire hit,
But still made a respectable profit.
It cannot claim to be my favourite –
I've never been sure what to make of it.
The book was the result of his visit
To America. If it disappoints,
Dickens himself thought "in a hundred points"
That it was the best of his books by far.
I must beg to differ, but there you are.

A Christmas Carol, though, it seems to me,
Is a triumph and few will disagree.
His earnings from the book were far from huge,
But the impact of Ebenezer Scrooge
Was wonderful and endures to this day.
I'm reluctant to give the plot away:
Prepare to be spooked, that's all I'll say.

Enough of Dickens' novels. His next one,
The rather difficult *Dombey and Son*,
He competed in 1848,
For now a convenient cut-off date.

Rhyming History

W. M. Thackeray

Another novelist to celebrate
Is young William Makepeace Thackeray.
Less popular than Dickens, in his day,
His enduring triumph, *Vanity Fair*,
Is a work of genius. Be aware:
The unscrupulous Becky Sharp, ruthless,
Vain and an accomplished adventuress,
Is a heroine ahead of her time.
Seductive, and a woman in her prime,
She will stop at nothing to have her way.
"Which of us," asked William Thackeray,
"Is happy in this world?" Well, who can say?

The Year of Revolutions

Much of Europe, in 1848,   **1848**
Was rocked by revolution. The fate
Of chancellors, ambassadors and kings
Hung in the balance. Scores of uprisings
Shocked the continent to its very core.
The lasting impact was hard to ignore.

Unrest in France

France was first. Revolution broke out
In Paris in February. The rout
(For rout it was) of King Louis Philippe
Gave cause for the Queen of England to weep.
Remember her visit to France with cheese,
And beer, to compare their family trees?

Public meetings, by order, if you please,
Of the King and Prime Minister Guizot,
Had been banned throughout France. This edict, though,
Was as far as they were supposed to go.

The Early Victorians

It appears you could not ban a banquet!
Protests, yes, but that was the sum of it.
So a 'public feast' was planned in Paris.
Cue: a major political crisis.

Citizens in their thousands flooded in
Around *l'église Sainte-Marie-Madeleine.*
Hundreds of barricades were erected.
With a suddenness no one expected,
And a virulence, the violence spread.

The government fell. Louis Philippe fled,
Disguised. He was lucky to keep his head.
The King and his family (Guizot too)
Took refuge in England. Palmerston's view –
Not shared by the Queen, who would rather wait –
Was that Louis Philippe should abdicate
And the new *régime* be given a chance.
'Pam' favoured, yes, a republican France!

Rhyming History

Why did Palmerston come down on the side
Of the revolution? You decide.
Was it his bitter distrust of Guizot,
A pesky, interfering so-and-so;
Or was it simply because, at present,
Alphonse de Lamartine, the 'President',
Was the likeliest fellow to forestall
The darkest and deadliest threat of all,
For Europe at large, a Communist *coup*?

Politics in France were a potent brew.
By the summer Lamartine had resigned,
His fragile authority undermined
By those of a more conservative bent.
A fresh wave of popular discontent
Then led to horrible scenes of bloodshed.
On the streets of Paris thousands lay dead,
As the brutal dictator, Cavaignac
(Lamartine's choice), drove the rebels back.

Palmerston, sad to say, turned a blind eye
To the killings. If you care to ask why,
His double standards are hard to deny.
Having welcomed Louis Philippe's downfall,
It appeared not to trouble him at all
That Lamartine's successor was far worse,
A bloodthirsty tyrant. It sounds perverse,
But his Lordship's mood could change by the day.
As long as Britain's interests held sway,
Palmerston would do things Palmerston's way.

Trouble in Spain

Far more than was generally supposed
By Europe's liberals, Pam was opposed
To revolution – but then again,
Not always! Witness the events in Spain.

The Early Victorians

In March the people rose up in Madrid.
Palmerston's response, active and rapid,
Was to advise the Spanish government
To deal with the forces of discontent
By amending their constitution.
What a nerve! Palmerston's 'solution'
Was dismissed by the Spanish out of hand.
The Madrid government, you understand,
Was repressive and uncompromising,
Cruel and barbaric. The uprising
Was quashed with the utmost brutality.
The PM and arch-reactionary,
Narváez, by emergency decree,
Behaved with unbending severity.
The Spanish press claimed a great victory
Over Palmerston, whose stock, at zero,
Was eclipsed by Narváez, their hero.

Germany, Hungary, Austria and Italy

So Pam attracted the veneration
Of liberals and the condemnation
Of conservatives! Reactionaries
In Germany had a witty reprise,
As follows: "*Hat der Teufel einen Sohn,*"
It ran, "*so ist er sicher Palmerston.*"*

Yet moves for a united Germany
Palmerston opposed. Rights of assembly
And freedom of speech, not surprisingly,
Were a bridge too far in his Lordship's book.
Nor did Hungary get a second look.

---

*"Should the devil have a son,
"His name is surely Palmerston."

Rhyming History

Under Kossuth, the Hungarians rose
To assert their independence. God knows,
It was high time. "We shall be slaves no more,"
They avowed, as they declared open war
On their Austrian 'masters'. Some success
They enjoyed, but Pam could not have cared less.
He believed in the Austrian Empire.
The Hungarians' fate, however dire,
Impressed him less than Habsburg unity.

Palmerston thus missed an opportunity
To stand up for justice and for liberty.
Yet when it came to unrest in Italy,
Palmerston hinted to Viscount Ponsonby –
The British Ambassador in Vienna,
Salt of the earth, a most excellent fella –
That the Austrians had no proper business
In Italy at all! I have to confess,
There are times when it's hard to follow the plot.

Europe was in turmoil, like it or not.
Palmerston may have tried to stop the rot,
But the pains he took had a hollow ring.
Democracy was a terrible thing!
Liberalism, nationalism
And (Heaven forfend) socialism
Were a recipe for strife and schism.

Unrest among the Czechs, Romanians,
Slovaks, Slovenes, Serbs and Ukrainians –
To say nothing of the Italians
And the broken, oppressed Hungarians –
Was a challenge to the supremacy
Of the Austrians. Astonishingly,
Von Metternich, their Chancellor of State
For decades, suffered a similar fate

To Guizot of France, forced into exile
In England. Indeed it seemed for a while
That he was finished. But in '51,
After many Austrian battles won,
The old mucker was back to do his worst.
Former Emperor Ferdinand the First
Had stepped down. Metternich found work to do
Advising his successor and nephew,
Emperor Franz Josef. The monarchy
Had weathered the storm. As in Germany,
The Netherlands, Belgium, Hungary
And Prussia, order was soon restored.
Disappointment was the rebels' reward –
Or worse, far worse: exile, torture or death.
Power to the people? Don't hold your breath.

Louis Napoleon Bonaparte

In France democracy gained a small foothold.
Cavaignac took a chance, encouraged, we're told,
By his burgeoning popularity
Among the French middle class, the *bourgeoisie*.
He held free elections for President,
One man, one vote. That was as far as it went:
No women, take note. Nonetheless, I should say,
An amazing development for its day.

Louis Napoleon Bonaparte, nephew
To Napoleon the First ('Boney' to you),
Was Cavaignac's main rival in the poll.
He promised the earth. Louis, on a roll,
Pledged enduring support for the family,
The old and the unemployed, for property
And for religion – a complete full house!
He proved to be a liar and a louse.
Within three years he'd staged a *coup d'état*.
We'll come to that. For now, he was a star.

Five and a half million votes he won,
To Cavaignac's one and a half. Deal done.
Louis Napoleon's place in the sun,
A rocky ride, lasted twenty-two years.
Like all the best political careers,
It was destined, of course, to end in tears.

A more peaceful Britain

So, out of the turmoil of '48,
There did emerge one 'democratic' state,
Albeit short-lived. In that seismic year,
What awesome events were unfolding here?
Very few indeed, to put it bluntly.
Great Britain remained a peaceful country,
An example to all Europe. How so?

For a tense few months it was touch and go.
The Chartist movement was alive and well,
Although less of a challenge, truth to tell,
Than ten years earlier. Corn Law Reform,
Despite whipping up a terrible storm
In government, offered to common folk
A new dawn. Your average working bloke,
Your family man, had less interest
In the staging of political protest
Than earning as much as he was able,
And working hard to put food on the table.

Factory and mining legislation

Driven through by that reforming Tory,
The tenacious Earl of Shaftesbury,
The Ten Hour Bill had passed into law.
Sensitive souls had been shocked to the core
By the awful stories his Lordship told
Of children, exhausted and blue with cold,

The Early Victorians

Weak with disease, tending unfenced machines,
Toiling from dawn to dusk – terrible scenes.
Five years before, with commendable skill,
Shaftesbury had piloted his Mines Bill,
In fourteen short weeks, through Parliament.
This outlawed the underground employment
Of all women, and children under ten.
So at long last, with the stroke of a pen,
Small boys were freed from labour in the mines.
The new law had teeth – imprisonment, fines
And a special mines inspectorate.
Many a poor mite reaped the benefit.

These were only piecemeal reforms, it's true,
But significant nonetheless. Faith grew
Among the weak and unrepresented,
The unemployed and the discontented,
That a better future was on its way.

A Chartist demonstration

The 10th of April was a fateful day.
It had not gone unnoticed that in France
The desperate rebels had seized their chance
To despatch the King and his government.
The threat to the Queen and Parliament
Was perceived to be imminent and real.
Chartism still enjoyed popular appeal,
Its leaders credible and organised.
Russell was nervous (I am not surprised),
But much to his credit he kept his cool.
He was well prepared. Lord John was no fool.

A protest rally on Kennington Green,
On a massive scale never before seen,
Had been planned by the Chartists. Their intent
Was to march from there to Parliament

Rhyming History

To present a petition. The fear,
Among ministers, as the day drew near,
Was of bloodshed and violent unrest.
Lord John's fortitude was put to the test.
Would the rally trigger revolution?
Would the threat be met with resolution?
Would the government or the Chartists win through?
The simple truth was that nobody knew.

The Chartist leaders announced in advance –
Here, I should say, they were taking a chance –
That expected numbers stood in excess
Of one hundred and fifty thousand. Bless!
This was the wildest overestimate,
But Russell had to take account of it.

There was serious talk of civil war.
The Queen and her children, two days before,
Had been shunted off to the Isle of Wight.
The family's prospects looked none too bright.
The Duke of Wellington (it's wonderful)
Thought Osborne House could be vulnerable,
Across the Solent, to naval attack.
The noble Duke had been invited back,
At the grand old age of seventy-eight,
To muster the troops and co-ordinate
A defensive strategy for London.

Some reckoned the measures were overdone:
7,000 from the military,
Including, can you believe, cavalry;
Some 4,000 police, all on standby;
And at least 80,000 (Lord knows why)
Special constables! Nobody's sure
Of exact numbers. There may have been more.
The latter, of course, were all volunteers,
Fellows from different classes one hears,

Each in his own way keen to 'have a go'
To protect and preserve the *status quo*.

Few were called upon. To widespread surprise,
The vast crowd failed to materialise.
A protest 20,000-strong, at most,
Was the best figure the Chartists could boast –
Little better than a spit and a cough.
The driving rain put hordes of people off,
A damp squib indeed. Feargus O'Connor,
Chartist leader and a man of honour,
Irish rebel and radical MP,
Spoke up for justice and democracy.

Feargus had assured the powers-that-be
That none of the insurgents would be armed.
He kept his word. No one that day was harmed.
The protesters, though, were somewhat alarmed

Rhyming History

To be met, on their way from Kennington,
By troops (under orders from Wellington)
Blocking their way over Westminster Bridge.
Did O'Connor not enjoy privilege,
As an MP, to come to Parliament
Unhindered? Was this not what freedom meant?

Apparently not. The rally dispersed,
Now a rabble. The Duke had done his worst.
The Chartist petition, as rehearsed,
Was allowed through, however – in a cab.
Yes, after much argument and conflab,
A taxi was ordered, can you believe!
Feargus, the petition up his sleeve,
Presented the precious document
To the Commons' clerks. He was well content
With the five million folk who had signed.
But he was later mortified to find
That his estimate again fell far short,
This time by some three million. In sport,
Many had subscribed fictitious names,
Trivial, light-hearted, just fun and games.
'Sir Robert Peel' rubbed shoulders with 'No Cheese'
And 'Mr Punch'. What a wonderful wheeze!

England had proved herself fit for the fray.
"We had our revolution yesterday,"
Wrote Prince Albert, "and it ended in smoke."
Chartism was dead, no word of a joke.

The death of Melbourne

In November a figure from the past,
Alone and melancholy, breathed his last.
Lord Melbourne (the Queen's beloved 'Lord M.')
Died a sad man. It's easy to condemn,
But as Queen Victoria's first PM

The Early Victorians

He could have made a better fist of it.
He was lazy, that's the true gist of it.
The young Queen adored him. They read, they walked,
They rode out together, they laughed, they talked –
But when it came down to affairs of state,
The idle Viscount (here I hesitate)
Did Victoria few favours. His 'skill'
(If that's the word) was to sugar the pill.
The Queen relied on Melbourne night and day,
Grumpy and sullen when he was away.

She was devastated when he resigned.
Fate must sometimes be cruel to be kind:
Their parting was the making of the Queen.
A grown woman, no longer eighteen,
She soon asserted her independence,
And with Albert's guidance quickly saw sense.

His Lordship went into steady decline.
A year after being forced to resign,
He suffered a stroke. He was sixty-three.
He would sit all day in his library,
An unread volume open on his knee,
Brooding on the past. Illness, loss of friends,
Loss of office... The Queen would make amends,
Sending her 'dear Lord M.' the odd letter.
This usually made him feel better,
But such favours were few and far between.

On those rare occasions he saw the Queen,
At a dinner or a social event,
He found it hard to hide his discontent
(Disappointment, rather) at the sad fact
That she had little to say. Out of tact,
Or kindness, her Majesty would converse...
About books... or the weather. Which was worse,

Rhyming History

The Viscount asked himself: to be ignored
Or to know his dear sovereign was bored?
Regret and sorrow were Melbourne's reward.
A comeback? If only. In '46,
He dreamt of a return to politics.

He travelled from Brocket Hall, Hertfordshire,
To a meeting of Whigs. He was on fire!
He spoke in support of Sir Robert Peel
And the issue that was to set the seal
On his premiership, Corn Law repeal.
Melbourne considered reform "a damn thing",
But to give Sir Robert a hammering
Would be short-sighted, opportunistic,
Discreditable and impolitic.

He carried his party with him. Good show!
But the Tory government had to go,
And when Peel fell (with the Corn Laws repealed)
Melbourne was confident he led the field
As his successor – or, if not PM,
Lord Privy Seal. The Queen's reply (a gem),
In the kindest of notes, was to explain
How she'd heard that his health was under strain,
So thought it best not to ask him again.

So Melbourne was never 'sent for'. Depressed,
Disappointed and easily distressed,
He acknowledged the truth. His day was done.
Old age and sickness are never much fun.
The poor chap became tetchy and fretful,
Prey to fits of worry, and forgetful.
At times his warmth and kindliness shone through,
The old William, good-humoured and true.

The dying days of 1848,
The 25th of November the date,

The Early Victorians

Brought Melbourne's distinguished life to a close.
He had drifted into a peaceful doze,
God bless him, from which he never awoke.
Six long years after suffering his stroke,
William Lamb, 2nd Viscount Melbourne, died.
He was buried, with Caroline by his side,
In Hatfield churchyard. The mourners were few.
Out with the old, they say, in with the new.
"A most kind and disinterested friend,"
Wrote Victoria, recording his end,
Whose loss she felt "truly and seriously".
So much for a fulsome obituary.

Violence in Ireland

Ireland was in turmoil. The murder rate,
In a year, had risen from sixty-eight
To ninety-six, that's well over a third.
A rise of sixty *per cent* had occurred
In firearms cases "with intent to slay".
Theft and arson were going the same way,
With armed assaults increasing by the day.
A growing taste for assassination,
The murder of landlords, gripped the nation.

One Major Mahon, caustic and cruel,
Had little time for paupers, as a rule.
He treated his tenants worse than vermin.
At the time of the potato famine,
He shipped nine hundred of them overseas.
Three hundred perished, many from disease,
Others from hunger. Mahon was denounced,
In church, and a sentence of death pronounced –
Not in so many words, you understand,
But tacit, unspoken and underhand.
He was, the priest declared, "worse than Cromwell"
Yet "this man lives". He was casting a spell.

Rhyming History

Two weeks later the Major met his end.
Such outrages were seen as a godsend
By hardliners, the likes of Palmerston
And the Lord Lieutenant, Lord Clarendon.
Both urged heavier fines, and an Arms Bill.
They harassed poor Russell, who'd had his fill.

He agreed that the murders were dreadful,
But wholesale ejectment, by the shedful,
Of tenants from their homes was also wrong.
Palmerston, of course, came on very strong.
The murders would soon end, like it or not,
If every time a landlord was shot
A priest was hanged in retaliation!
People were slow in their condemnation –
This was Palmerston, popular hero:
For bigotry, ten; common sense, zero.

The Cabinet, fatally divided,
Fighting like dogs, remained undecided.
Little was accomplished to keep the peace.
Russell's misgivings were on the increase
Throughout the heady days of '48.
Civil war, too dreadful to contemplate,
Was nonetheless a frightening prospect.
Yet, contrary to what you might expect,
The Irish rebellion fizzled out.
A lack of strategy, without a doubt,
Contributed. So Ireland muddled on,
No thanks to Clarendon or Palmerston.

A royal visit to Ireland

To mark the end of the four-year famine,   **1849**
Queen Victoria visited Dublin.
This was a risk, to be sure. Clarendon
Expressed himself as nervous as Lord John,

But the Irish tour was a great success.
"Cork looks rather foreign," wrote the Queen (bless!).
"The crowd is very good-humoured, running
"And pushing about, laughing and talking
"And shrieking." She drove round "without escort,"
According to Lord Clarendon's report.
Victoria was not the nervous sort.

Eight days her visit lasted. The Irish
Were a people the Queen came to cherish.
During the lamentable famine years,
The plight of the hungry moved her to tears.
She gave generously to charity.
One wicked and disgraceful calumny
Implied that she donated just five pounds,
Quite as mean and insulting as it sounds,
To the cause of Irish famine relief –
A vicious slander beyond belief.

Rhyming History

Her contribution to the starving poor
Was two thousand pounds, quite possibly more.

She subscribed to other charities too.
It was not for governments, in her view,
To support good causes, but such as she.
She jeopardised her popularity
Among the middle classes, the wealthy
And the self-obsessed aristocracy,
By intimating that they could do more.

Well, so be it. She didn't give a straw.
The generous sums that the Queen did give
To worthy causes were proof positive
Of her good heart. She gave fifteen *per cent*
Of her private income. Magnificent!
Noble, public-spirited and decent.

Gunboat diplomacy

Lord Palmerston was up to his old tricks.
Prone to fine displays of histrionics –
Wellington called them bullying tactics –
His Lordship tended to go overboard,
Flaunting Britain's authority abroad.
Our naval and military strength
Was vast. This Pam would go to any length
To broadcast. So didn't people know it!
What use was power if not to show it?
This was popular. His fans, by and large,
Were more than happy the Brits were in charge.
Gunboat diplomacy is what it's called.
Britain was ready. The Queen was appalled.

Palmerston preferred to shoot from the hip.
Trouble abroad? Send in a battleship!

The Don Pacifico affair

It was the case of Don Pacifico
That brought matters to a head. This fellow
Hailed from Portugal, a middle-aged Jew,
But (among Portuguese) one of the few
Who were blessed with British citizenship.
His parents, it seemed, had taken a trip
To Gibraltar, which is where he was born.
Had his mother given birth in Runcorn,
He could not have been more British. The law
Was the law: he was a Brit to the core.

Years later our hero fetched up in Greece.
He found himself in trouble with the police,
But that was altogether by the by.
Don Pacifico may have been small fry
And a bit of a menace – nonetheless,
He was British. This, I have to confess,
Was awkward, but that was the crux of it.

Fair to say, he did not think much of it
When his home, attacked by a racist mob,
Was razed to the ground, a most thorough job.
All his wealth and worldly goods were destroyed.
Don Pacifico, far from overjoyed,
Called for the Athens cops to be deployed.
When they arrived they stood for three hours
Watching the blaze. So much for police powers.

Don Pacifico, the dispossessed Jew,
Put in a massive claim (well, wouldn't you?)
For over twenty-seven thousand pounds,
Based, I regret, on pretty flimsy grounds.
For his case was not as strong as it sounds.
A large proportion of the sum 'owing'
Was for lost documents. There was no knowing

Whether these had ever existed at all.
Was he banging his head against a brick wall?

The government of Greece declined to act.
They stated, as undeniable fact,
That no racial prejudice existed
In Greece. Don Pacifico persisted,
But the Greeks refused, categorically,
To support his claim. Now it seems to me
That the police had behaved disgracefully,
And that some measure of compensation
Was surely due. A tricky situation.

Don Pacifico wrote to Palmerston:
He was "of the Jewish religion"
And "an English subject". He sought, as such,
The benefit of his Lordship's magic touch

The Early Victorians

To compel the Greeks "to perform a duty…
"Of equity". The letter was a beauty.
It evoked the need for "a firm will… a strong hand…"
In language only Palmerston would understand.

It took Pam two years, believe it or not,
Before he determined to stop the rot.
But in December, 1849,
He finally resolved to draw the line.
He wrote to the British Minister, Wyse –
The missive came as a nasty surprise –
Requiring him to seek satisfaction
Of the Greeks, and threatening swift action
From the British Mediterranean fleet.
The Greek government began to feel the heat.

In January the demand was made.   **1850**
Thirty-one thousand pounds were to be paid,
With three years' interest at twelve *per cent*.
It appears that Palmerston was hell-bent
On rubbing the Greeks' noses in the dirt.
The last demand, which must surely have hurt,
Was that payment was due within a day –
Yes, twenty-four hours! I do have to say
This was crazy, but it was Palmerston's way.

The money was unforthcoming of course.
Lord Palmerston's critics yelled themselves hoarse,
But to no avail. A Greek ship was seized.
Her captain and crew were highly displeased,
But they surrendered without resistance.
What else could they do? At Pam's insistence,
The port of Piraeus was blockaded.
Just as hopes of a compromise faded,
The French, bless 'em, offered to mediate.
The great blockade, pending further debate,

Rhyming History

Was suspended. But Palmerston forgot
To tell Wyse! Was this on purpose… or not?
It seems unlikely, but I'm curious.

The French, in the meantime, were furious.
There were two completely separate deals.
Palmerston of course, deaf to all appeals,
Stood by Wyse. There was even talk of war –
War with France. What on earth was it all for?
Largely to satisfy Palmerston's pride.
He'd given the Greeks a pretty rough ride,
But now had the gall to dub the affair
Just "a slight scrimmage". Russell didn't dare
Confront him, and the Queen was unaware,
At first, of his Lordship's orders to Wyse
To seize Greek shipping. Cut him down to size?
Victoria tried. She met with Russell.
Pam's displays of diplomatic muscle
Were not to her taste. Lord John's position
Was not dissimilar. Palmerston's mission
Was "hardly worth the interposition
"Of the British Lion". Very well said.

Yet he did nothing. It came to a head
In mid-July when Stanley, in the Lords,
Moved a vote of censure. Pam had crossed swords
With Stanley in the past. Now Palmerston
Had overreached himself. His day was done.

Or was it? His whole foreign policy
Had been denounced. By a majority
Of thirty-seven the censure motion
Was carried. Aware of the commotion,
Palmerston informed the government of France
That Britain was backing down. He'd had his chance
And had blown it. Don Pacifico's claim
Would be put to arbitration. Pam's name,

The Early Victorians

For once, was mud. It was highly provoking
For Don Pacifico, though it's worth noting
That his damages were finally assessed
At one hundred and fifty pounds! I'm impressed.
In those distant days that was no mean sum.
I've a strong feeling that justice was done.

As for the unfortunate Palmerston,
He tendered his resignation. Well,
Lord John would not accept it. Truth to tell,
Russell knew that this was a watershed.
His Whig government was as good as dead
Should Palmerston fall. It made perfect sense
To arrange for a vote of confidence
In the Commons. The beleaguered Palmerston
He hailed as a fine colleague, second to none,
And "the Minister of England". Credit that!
If Pam could weather the storm, I'll eat my hat.

The Commons debate stretched over four nights,
For Palmerston the most famous of fights.
He emerged triumphant, from what I hear:
The most rousing speech of his long career.
The motion was won by forty-six votes.
Speaking for over four hours, with few notes,
He reviewed his whole foreign policy.
The British had shown that "liberty
"Is compatible with order". He spoke
On behalf of plain, honest, common folk,
Who simply sought freedom under the law.

Then the climax. Just as in days of yore
A Roman would be entitled to say,
"*Civis Romanus sum*" – proof, in his day,
Of the constitutional guarantee
Of his rights and freedom from indignity –

Rhyming History

So also should your average British guy
Enjoy confidence in England's "watchful eye"
And her "strong arm" to protect him from "wrong
"And injustice". Palmerston was on song.
In vain did others seek to make the case
Against him. That highly privileged race,
The Romans, were accomplished oppressors.
It was all very well, as aggressors,
For the state to enforce the liberties
Of its citizens. The Peels, the Disraelis
And the Gladstones made little or no impact.
It was Palmerston's triumph, and that's a fact.

He was cheered to the rooftops. A portrait
Was commissioned by his fans, first-rate
And a fine likeness, from one John Partridge –
Whose namesake, as you know, it's my privilege
To call a friend, an artist in his prime.
Partridge was celebrated in his time
For his paintings in oil. Second to none,
His brilliant study of Palmerston
Was presented to his wife, Lady P.
She was thrilled, accepting it graciously.

Pam got off very lightly, it seems to me.
But his luck could not last, as soon we shall see.

In the great Don Pacifico debate,
Many a political heavyweight
Inveighed against Palmerston's policy.
Sir Robert Peel, famed for his honesty
And thorough good sense, was more reflective.
From an ex-Prime Minister's perspective,
He was able to command the respect
Of the Commons and, as you would expect,
Delivered a wise and temperate speech.
Britain's role in the world was not to preach,

Nor to dictate to other nations.
International relations
Were best served by non-intervention.

It was not Sir Robert's intention
To bring down the government. His desire
Was simply to show that those who aspire
To "constitutional liberty"
Do so best "by their own efforts". To me,
This is the essence of diplomacy.
Sir Robert's words were the epitome
Of a far-sighted foreign policy.

Death of Sir Robert Peel.

The following morning dawned clear and bright,
A busy day ahead, to Peel's delight.
First, a meeting of the Commission
On the forthcoming Exhibition;
Then to his study in the afternoon;
And finally, not a moment too soon
(For this he loved), his customary ride
At five o'clock. Peel was well satisfied
That his mount, a recent acquisition,
Was a fine horse, in tip-top condition.
His son-in-law had recommended the beast,
Good-tempered and steady, a comfort at least.

It later transpired that the wretched horse –
Dozens came forward to say so, of course –
Had a reputation for kicking.
What happened next was simply sickening.
At the top of Constitution Hill,
A stone's throw from St. George's Hospital,
The horse bucked, throwing Peel over its head,
Hard to the ground. His life hung by a thread.

The horse then fell on him, striking his back.
He blacked out. Sir Robert was on the rack.

They carried him home in hideous pain.
He recovered consciousness again,
But the fracture of his left collar bone,
And a number of his ribs – these alone
Were agony. It was ripped cartilage
And a massive internal haemorrhage
That hastened the crisis. The Prince, no less,
Paid his respects, in a state of distress.

The Duke of Wellington made two visits.
The sickroom, to most, was beyond limits,
But outside Whitehall Gardens the crowds grew.
Peel was the people's friend, and this they knew.

The Early Victorians

They gathered in silence, plain working folk.
Corn Law reform, Sir Robert's masterstroke,
Had changed their lives. Bread they could now afford.
It is little wonder Peel was adored.

Three days after the accident he died.
In the Lords, Wellington broke down and cried.
He spoke of Sir Robert's passion for truth.
Never, even in the days of his youth,
Had he been known to utter one word
That he did not fully believe. Absurd,
For a man in public life? Wellington
Should surely be trusted, if anyone.

"A great light" (this the Earl of Aberdeen)
"Has disappeared from amongst us." The Queen
Was moved to write to her uncle to say,
"Poor dear Peel is to be buried today".
She had trouble keeping her tears at bay.
"The sorrow and grief at his death," she wrote,
"Are most touching. The country mourns" (I quote)
"Over him as over a father." Yes,
A feeling of overwhelming sadness
Swept the nation. It was raining hard
As they laid him to rest. In the churchyard,
And the wide expanse of park and woodland
Around Drayton, mourners stood, hand in hand,
Country labourers, workmen with their wives
And little children. The record survives.

Shops closed their shutters, flags flew at half mast,
The mills locked their gates as folk stood aghast,
Shocked to the core, barely able to speak.
The French Assembly (this was unique),
In due deference to the 'Peel effect',
Suspended their sitting out of respect.

Sir Robert Peel, aged sixty-two, was dead.
The mighty *Times* hit the nail on the head:
"The greatest statesman of his time," it said.

The Great Exhibition

On the 1st of May, 1851,   **1851**
The wonderful Great Exhibition
Opened in Hyde Park. As well as huge fun,
It was a grand and momentous affair.
It seems the whole world and his wife were there.
Some 700,000 loyal folk
Lined the royal route, no word of a joke,
From Buckingham Palace. Victoria –
Her mood was one of high euphoria –
Was moved by the vast crowds. The Park was filled
"As far as the eye could reach". She was thrilled
By the gleaming "gigantic edifice"
As her glance fell on the 'Crystal Palace'.

Joseph Paxton's structure had been so called
By *Punch*. Critics and cynics were appalled
By other designs. One was by Brunel,
A long, brick building, a vision of hell,
Surmounted by a clumsy iron dome
As big, we're told, as St. Peter's in Rome!
A further two hundred and thirty-three
Had been rejected by the Committee.
Time was short. It was coming to the crunch.
Isambard's plans were the best of the bunch.

Joseph Paxton

William Ellis MP had a hunch.
He entertained Joseph Paxton to lunch.
We met Paxton in 1843,
When the Queen and Albert took a journey

The Early Victorians

To Chatsworth. They admired the 'Great Stove',
Joseph's 'house of glass'. A clever young cove,
Gardener, architect and engineer,
He was nothing if not a pioneer.

Within days of his meeting with Ellis,
Paxton put the Committee on notice
With doodles on his blotter, his sketches
For a new design: glass panes (great stretches)
In a cast-iron framework. Its main strength
Was its huge scale – two thousand feet in length
And some four hundred and fifty feet wide,
With a height of one hundred and nine feet
At the transept. The designs were complete
Within a week, a remarkable feat.

The Committee, with a sigh of relief,
Snapped up his plan. Others (beyond belief)
Still cavilled and carped. Colonel Sibthorpe –
Lost, according to some, in a time warp –
Objected to Hyde Park as a venue.
It was his not unreasonable view
That trees would have to be felled to make way
For the monstrous edifice. For his day,
The Colonel's concerns, I have to say,
Were laudable. Trees matter, as we know.

Paxton's answer to this, as answers go,
Was a gem. The elm trees were left to grow
Within the building! The only slight hitch,
One that sadly threatened to queer his pitch,
Were the little birds that lived in the trees.
Their 'droppings' would cause havoc, if you please,
To the treasures and exhibits below.
What was to be done? Well, what do you know?
The Queen herself (on Prince Albert's behalf)
Consulted Wellington. You have to laugh.

"Sparrowhawks, ma'am," was the old man's advice.
The problem, at source, was solved in a trice.
For the birdies, of course, not quite so nice.

Henry Cole

The brains behind the Great Exhibition
Was Henry Cole. The Royal Commission
Was Cole's idea. An administrator
Of genius, a couple of years before
He had troubled to take a trip overseas,
To Paris, with some fellow dignitaries
From the Society of Arts, for a glance
At what Britain's rivals were up to in France.

He was impressed, but thought we could do better.
Great Britain was already a trend-setter
In science, invention, art and design.
An Exhibition, a palpable sign
Of the craft and talent of the nation,
Would constitute a great celebration
Of Britain's liberal spirit and Free Trade.
Cole's colleagues agreed and the case was made.

Prince Albert was persuaded to take the chair
Of the Royal Commission, well aware
That he and its members were taking a risk.
They had seventeen months. They'd better be brisk.
Where would the money come from? Parliament
Had registered a measure of discontent,
By refusing to commit one penny piece.
The project clearly needed some elbow grease.
Subscriptions of five thousand pounds apiece
Came from Lord Granville and Henry Labouchere,
Committee members both. Cole showed a great flair
For fundraising. Samuel Morton Peto,
A financier and a splendid fellow,

The Early Victorians

Contributed fifty thousand pounds, no less,
A vote of confidence, I have to confess,
Beyond anybody's expectation.

Prince Albert, on behalf of the nation,
Raised the balance of funds from private backers –
Well in excess of eighty thousand smackers.

A spectacular success

Cynics still reckoned the project was crackers.
The Crystal Palace would harbour foreign spies,
Agitators from France. To no one's surprise,
This proved to be a myth. Others held the view
That the working classes (this was nothing new)
Would be drunk, disorderly and violent.
Remember the Chartists? No experiment
Could be more dangerous. This fear also proved
Unfounded. Indeed, the public were much moved
By the good behaviour of all classes.
Admission prices varied. Day passes
From Monday to Thursday cost just one shilling,
Five bob on Saturdays (if you were willing)
And on Fridays you could go for half a crown.
The trick of keeping the ticket prices down
Encouraged six million visits (it's true)
Before the Great Exhibition closed. Phew!

All classes alike were full of good cheer.
"Who'd ever have thought of meeting you here?"
Ran the caption under a *Punch* cartoon,
As one family had the good fortune
To bump into their lower-class neighbours.
They were all smiles. The tireless labours
Of Cole and the Prince were vindicated,
As the British public celebrated

Rhyming History

A national triumph. One issue
That taxed the organisers: what to do
When people needed to go to the loo?
'Retiring rooms' were built with this in mind,
A great novelty, I think you will find.

These 'facilities', as good as any,
Were open to all and cost one penny –
Hence, 'to spend a penny'. It's my belief
That some 800,000 sought relief
From these temporary lavatories –
Yet another of the success stories
Associated with this great event.

What of the Exhibition's content?
Over 100,000 exhibits –
I cannot list them all, space prohibits –
Were on display, both British and foreign.
Cheek by jowl with the newest steam engine
Stood a *papier mâché* fire screen
From Spiers and Sons; and from Roger and Dean
A fine bedstead carved out of walnut wood.
Then Rodgers and Sons of Sheffield came good
With their huge so-called 'Crystal Palace' knife,
With eighty blades (you could fear for your life),
Each inlaid with delicate gold etching
And superb engravings, representing
Windsor Castle and Osborne House (a wealth
Of detail) and the Crystal Palace itself.

This was one in the eye for the philistines.
There was a wide range of up-to-date designs,
Like microscopes, cameras and steam turbines,
All along the latest scientific lines.
To prevent some visitors becoming bored,
There were thousands of exhibits from abroad:

French silks and German toys (squirrels playing whist,
Dolls at a garden *fête* – well, you get the gist);
A Chinese room, with lanterns, fans and tea;
A large column of silver filigree,
A form of ornamental tracery
(Try to imagine), from Sardinia;
Cottons, silks and satins from India;
Even (from Canada) snow shoes and sleighs.

The 'Albertopolis'

The show was calculated to amaze.
The Crystal Palace proved a massive hit.
The Exhibition showed a profit
Of just under two hundred thousand pounds,
A figure as impressive as it sounds.
Henry Cole and the Prince used the surplus
To purchase, with the minimum of fuss,

Rhyming History

The South Kensington Estate. It is this
That has been dubbed the 'Albertopolis' –
Housing the Royal Colleges of Art,
Of Music and of Organists. Some start!
They founded the Science Museum too,
The Victoria and Albert (that's two)
And a third, the Natural History.
How they found the time is a mystery –
Or the energy. For that was not all.
What was later the Royal Albert Hall
Was part of this extraordinary plan.
Henry Cole was a remarkable man.
The Imperial College of Science
Was also his – well, he raised the finance.

Sir Henry, in his quiet, modest way,
Was a great Victorian. Sad to say,
There are few who remember his name today.

The new Crystal Palace

A footnote. After six months' wild success,
And unanimous plaudits from the press,
The Crystal Palace was relocated
To Sydenham Hill. Recalibrated
And extended – its barrel-vaulted roof
And two huge transepts were visible proof –
The new Palace had a vast concert hall
That could seat 4,000 people in all.
The scale was breathtaking. Folk were in thrall.

It took ten times the original cost
To make the move. Serious sums were lost.
Yet the Palace hosted an entire range
Of entertainments, some novel, some strange.
Charles Blondin, the famous tightrope walker
And celebrated circus performer,

The Early Victorians

Gave a demonstration of his art
On the high wire. Such frolics apart,
The Crystal Palace hosted pantomime
(*Dick Whittington*) and, a first for its time,
A cat show (separate from the panto,
Which featured a cat, as I'm sure you know).
Shakespeare galas, aeronautical shows,
Hockey on ice... The phrase 'anything goes'
Is the one that readily springs to mind.

The Crystal Palace steadily declined,
Over the years, in popularity,
Attendance and profitability.
In the early twentieth century
It fell into a state of disrepair.
The building wore a faintly shabby air
And suffered from a kind of atrophy.
The crisis came with the catastrophe
Of the fire of 1936.
An amazing show of pyrotechnics,
The blaze was no scheduled entertainment.
The flames (no question of containment)
Quickly spread. There was a strong wind that night.
The old timber floor boards were soon alight.

They saw the Crystal Palace burning bright
Across seven counties, an awesome sight.
The mighty structure was razed to the ground
Within hours. I dare say, pound for pound,
The British public got their money's worth.
Little more now than a patch of charred earth,
It had served them proudly over the years.
90,000 Londoners, some in tears,
Were witness to the great conflagration,
One a future leader of the nation,
Winston Churchill, no less. "This is the end,"
He said, "of an age." Truth is a bitter friend.

Palmerston dismissed

Lord Palmerston soon got his come-uppance.
The old scoundrel had never cared tuppence
For his critics. Russell he detested.
Pam's patience had been sorely tested
Over the Don Pacifico affair.
Lord John's support, as he was well aware,
Had been driven by pure self-interest,
The policy designed to serve him best.
Russell was wary. Pam, under attack,
Was dangerous. Johnny should watch his back.

Palmerston's fall from grace, oddly enough,
Was a French affair. It was heady stuff.
The presidential election
Of '48 had been handsomely won

The Early Victorians

By Boney's nephew, Louis Napoleon.
So far, so good. But in 1851,
In December, he staged a *coup d'état.*
For the British this was one step too far.
Another Emperor Napoleon?
Heaven forfend! The Duke of Wellington,
Strangely, approved (why, I have no idea),
But Lord John Russell's Cabinet was clear:
A strict neutrality should be maintained.
Little, if anything, was to be gained
From jumping the gun. Palmerston, it seems,
Agreed with his colleagues. Well, in your dreams!

Pam was all for the *coup.* Napoleon –
He alone, according to Palmerston –
Could save the French from socialism.
It was this spirit of optimism
That prompted him to ask Count Walewski,
The French envoy in London, instantly
To pass his sincere congratulations
To Louis Napoleon. Relations
Between Palmerston and our man in Paris,
Normanby, plunged to rock bottom over this.
The British policy of neutrality,
As announced by Ambassador Normanby,
Was directly at odds with Palmerston's views.

To Normanby this was most unwelcome news.
He had no time for his Lordship anyway,
With very good cause, I am tempted to say.
He complained to Lord John. His indignant wife
Took it up with the Queen. You can bet your life,
Victoria was furious. Poor Lord John.
He had no choice but to confront Palmerston.
Pam shrugged the matter off. As the PM knew,
He was only expressing a private view,
No more, no less. This was patently untrue –

Rhyming History

Smoke and mirrors. It was the end of the line
For Palmerston. Of course, he failed to resign,
So Russell bit the bullet and dismissed him.
Pam, to be sure, had acted on no mere whim.
To him it was all a bit of a lark.
Foreign affairs were a walk in the park,
But for once he had overstepped the mark.
Old Pam's career was as good as dead.
"There *was* a Palmerston," Disraeli said.

Never believe it! This was Chapter One
Of *The Fall and Rise of Lord Palmerston*.

'Pam' takes his revenge

Within two months Lord P, the dirty rat,   **1852**
Accomplished what he called his "tit-for-tat
"With Johnny Russell". In February,
With Lord John's government rightly wary
Of France's military might, a Bill
To address this new and deadly peril
Was introduced on the floor of the House.
Pam, the opportunistic little louse,
Quickly tabled a wrecking amendment,
Strongly opposing the establishment
Of local militia. In their place,
He pulled out the stops and argued the case
For a national militia. Well,
With Lord Palmerston raising merry hell,
He managed to bring the Tories on side.

John Russell was defeated. Far and wide
The relief was palpable. For six years
Johnny had soldiered on. Tantrums, tears
And temper were the order of the day.
Little was achieved, to widespread dismay.

There were few regrets. He was not much missed.
Capricious, wilful (you get the gist),
Ill-mannered, muddled and irresolute,
It was high time John was given the boot.

The 14th Earl of Derby

The Earl of Derby was the next PM.
It is harder to praise than to condemn,
But the 14th Earl was a mere stopgap.
A relaxed, amiable sort of chap,
His government lasted less than a year.
Accomplishments early in his career
Included an Education Act
For Ireland, piloted through with some tact.
This is the legal basis, to this day,
For most Irish primary schools. I should say
Though no expert, that in its own modest way
This was quite a feat. In 1834,
As the youthful Lord Stanley, he oversaw
The Abolition of Slavery Act,
A significant triumph, and that's a fact.

He started his career as an ardent Whig,
Then switched to the Tories. He cared not a fig
What people thought. Indeed, he changed sides again –
Twice! Derby was blessed with a brilliant brain,
Yet he clashed with Peel. I had better explain.
Though Tory (for the second time), he opposed
The repeal of the Corn Laws. His mind was closed
To the manifest benefits of free trade.
He clung to the past. What a mistake he made.
He broke from Sir Robert Peel, the Tories split,
And for a generation that was it.
The Protectionist wing of the party,
Led by the aforementioned Lord Derby –

Rhyming History

In the landowning interest, hence his stand
On Corn Law reform – held a very weak hand.
They could never command a majority
In Parliament. Derby's authority
Was circumscribed from day one. It's no surprise
That the Peelites would offer no compromise.
Derby and the Corn Law rebels, in their eyes,
Prioritised their interests over those
Of the party, and such treachery, God knows,
Was unforgivable. What could Derby do?

Precious little, it seems. In '52
His new ministry was nicknamed the 'Who? Who?' –
After the Duke of Wellington, bless his heart,
Nodded off in the Lords, awoke with a start,
And exclaimed, "Who? Who?" as the names were read out
Of Derby's ministers. There was little doubt
That the government would struggle to survive.
In a futile attempt to keep it alive,
Lord Derby called a summer election.
The voters returned a broad cross-section
Of MPs – dozens more conservatives, true,
But Whigs, Peelites, Irish and radicals too.
Still with no majority, what could he do?
Soldier on! Old Derby became PM
Three times – but it was forever 'us' and 'them',
The former the minority. Poor chap,
It seems he stumbled from mishap to mishap.
Second and third times round he would achieve more,
But in '52 Derby's record was poor.

His Chancellor was Benjamin Disraeli.
Dizzy's rise to power in time we shall see,
But he proved himself a mediocrity
In this, Derby's first administration.
His budget, to widespread consternation,
Was defeated by a combination

Of the aforesaid Irish, Whigs and Peelites –
Not, I fear, the most edifying of fights.
This led in December to Derby's collapse.
As catastrophes go, not the worst perhaps.

The death of Wellington

Celebrated by Alfred Tennyson,
The poet, as "the last great Englishman",
The famous 'Iron Duke' of Wellington
Slipped peacefully away in September.

As well as the great victor, remember,
Of Waterloo, the Duke was a statesman
Of considerable weight. Wellington
Lent his support to emancipation
For Catholics – something of a *volte-face*,
Given his personal views on the Mass.

Rhyming History

Never afraid of a gathering storm,
He gave his backing to Corn Law reform.
He stood by Sir Robert. He disagreed
With Peel, but in Britain's hour of need
He backed repeal. He owed it to the Queen.
Though prone to snoozing in the Lords (as we've seen),
It was his bounden duty to intervene.
Loyalty was the Iron Duke's middle name,
Military genius his claim to fame.
Waterloo was "a damned close-run thing," he swore.
The battle was fought to the death, to be sure,
But Wellington's Army showed Boney the door.

The noble Duke was eighty-three when he died.
Victoria was bereft. Oh, how she cried.
The Duke's body lay in state in the Great Hall,
All decked out in black, of Chelsea Hospital.
Thousands came to pay their respects. In the rush
To file past, a number were killed in the crush.
Over a million mourners lined the route
To St. Paul's, a fitting and moving tribute
To a most extraordinary statesman.
In the crypt, next to Admiral Lord Nelson,
He was laid to rest. "Our immortal hero,"
The grieving Queen called him. Whether friend or foe,
Few could quarrel with what *The Times* had to say:
The Duke's life was "one unclouded longest day".

Lord Aberdeen

The new Prime Minister was Aberdeen,
A long-standing favourite with the Queen.
At the Foreign Office, as we have seen,
Under Peel, he scored major successes –
In contrast to Palmerston's excesses –
With America, France and Tahiti.
An outstanding diplomat, it was he,

The Early Victorians

Aberdeen, to universal surprise,
Who finally brokered a compromise
Over the vexed and smouldering issue
Of the Spanish marriages. It's true,
To give the wretched Palmerston his due,
That Spain turned the tables. It was absurd,
However, when the Spanish broke their word,
To blame Aberdeen. He rose to the test.
He behaved with honour and did his best.

His fledgling government was heady stuff.
The Peelite Tories were not strong enough
To go it alone. It was Whig support
That Aberdeen needed and this he sought.
Within months of being given the sack
(Can you credit this?), Palmerston was back –
Incongruously, at the Home Office.
An opportunity too good to miss:
A return to power. His former post,
The one in his heart he coveted most,
Was barred, given his recent track record.
The Queen vetoed it. Was Palmerston bored,
Saddled with home affairs? Far from it.
He proved himself remarkably fit –
Eager, enterprising and energised.

Palmerston's domestic achievements

His critics were agreeably surprised
To find him seeking a solution
To the scourge of river pollution.
By the Factory Act of '53,
He showed an unexpected energy
As a reformer, improving the lot
Of the younger worker. Like it or not,
Palmerston was a progressive. The smoke,
In towns and cities, was beyond a joke.

Rhyming History

Palmerston moved a Smoke Abatement Bill.
The proposed measure proved a bitter pill
To the 'personal freedom' brigade. Still,
His Lordship's reforms were a welcome start
And appeared at least to come from the heart.

Fortune smiled on Palmerston. Home affairs
Were to prove the answer to his prayers.
He watched as Aberdeen, caught unawares
In the quicksand of the Crimean War,
Died a slow death. Palmerston knew the score.
The public could hardly hold him to blame.
At the Foreign Office he'd made his name,
But he was responsible no longer.
Pam could thus emerge fitter and stronger
As Aberdeen's successor. This he knew.
Sit tight. It was all he needed to do.

Lord Russell at the Foreign Office

That other pillar of the Whig party,
Lord John Russell, the right little smarty,
Was named as new Foreign Secretary.
Was old Aberdeen acting recklessly?
Wee Lord John, it was undeniable,
Was flaky, weak and unreliable,
More than ready at the drop of a hat
To resign from Cabinet. Add to that,
If you will, the unpalatable fact
That he made the oddest sort of contract
With the Prime Minister: only to serve
In this office for two months. What a nerve!
Leadership of the Commons he preferred
And this post, he gave Aberdeen his word,
He would be happy to occupy. Well,
John reckoned himself a bit of a swell.

The Early Victorians

Young William Gladstone

Aberdeen's government, don't get me wrong,
On paper at least, looked stable and strong.
William Gladstone, a fellow Peelite,
Moral, loyal and formidably bright,
Was his new Chancellor. Aged forty-three,
And a breath of fresh air, take it from me,
Gladstone's first budget made a great impact,
A fine political *début* in fact.
There was no going back. The case was made,
And would never be reversed, for Free Trade.
Even young Disraeli, in a rare fit
Of humility, saw the good in it.

So: a Cabinet brimming with good sense,
Talent and a wealth of experience,
Led by a man of strong intelligence
And purpose. All was set fair to succeed.

The Crimea

What price Fortune in your hour of need?
Trouble was brewing in the Crimea.
Imminent war? The very idea…
Yet storm clouds were gathering fast, for sure.
Religion (often the final straw)
Lay at the heart of it. Tsar Nicholas,
Tyrannical, autocratic and crass,
Had long had his eagle eye on Turkey –
The 'sick man of Europe'. Diplomacy
Interested him not a jot. The key
To the Holy Places in Palestine –
Bethlehem was a particular shrine –
Was the *casus belli*, ostensibly.
The case was handled far from sensibly.

Rhyming History

Eastern Orthodox Christianity
Within the Ottoman Empire (Turkey)
Was under Russian protection.

France, for one, voiced a strong objection
To the Tsar's claim to be the guardian
Of every orthodox Christian –
Ten million of them, can you believe –
In the Ottoman. Who was more naive,
Russia or France? Napoleon's case
(The Third of that name, a perfect disgrace)
Was that France enjoyed an historic right,
For which his people were ready to fight,
To exercise Latin sovereignty –
A western, Catholic authority –
Over the said Holy Places. Turkey,
For her sins, faced a cruel dilemma.

The Sultan, a weak-willed sort of fella,
Gave in to French demands. A silver star
Was affixed (most surely a step too far)
By the French clergy in the very place
Where God Incarnate, in a state of grace,
Was born – namely, the Bethlehem manger.

The real cause of the conflict

This posed an unacceptable danger
To Greek and Russian orthodoxy.
The 'war', of course, was by way of proxy:
The main message that France was putting out –
Her true intention, no shadow of doubt –
Was that should the Russians take a chance,
And ever try to steal a march on France
In the sad event of Turkey's demise,
The Tsar would be in for a big surprise.

While the Holy Places were critical,
The issue, in truth, was political.
Nicholas's imperialist dreams
Were no secret. Napoleon, it seems,
Would be standing by with a show of force,
Should the Tsar overstep the mark. Of course,
Neither was prepared to make the first move.

Hostilities were kept at one remove
By focusing on the Holy Places.
The Tsar put the Sultan through his paces:
Authority over the Holy Land
Lay in the east. It's hard to understand
Why the Sultan continued to swither,
But Abd-el Medjid, all of a-dither,
Changed his tune. Russia did have a right
To the Holy Places! He was forthright

Rhyming History

In his support of the Tsar's counterclaim.
What did they think this was? Some kind of game?
Napoleon responded, to his shame,
By sending the battleship *Charlemagne*
To sail through the Dardanelles – quite insane,
A link in the inevitable chain
That led to war. What did the Sultan do?
He handed the keys (amazing, but true)
To the Holy Church of the Nativity,
In Bethlehem, to the French – a victory,
Heaven help us, for gunboat diplomacy.

Aberdeen's position

Tsar Nicholas the First was furious.
What of Britain? I'm only curious.
The new Prime Minister, Lord Aberdeen,
Was a man of peace. He was less than keen
On fuelling the flames. Russell, he knew,
Was a Cabinet hawk, Palmerston too.
They were more than prepared to go to war
To protect the Turks. Aberdeen forbore,
At this early stage, to express a view.
He would wait and see. What else could he do?

His Lordship had no fondness for Turkey:
"I despise the Turks," he told friends firmly.
The government was the "most oppressive
"In all the world". This was unimpressive,
Given the current dangerous context.
The Tsar, it seemed, would use any pretext
To exploit the vulnerability
Of the poor Turks. It is easy to see
Why he put his faith in the new PM.
He viewed it as a case of 'us' and 'them'.
So simple: let Russia and Britain
Join forces to carve up the Ottoman!

What of Johnny Russell and Palmerston?
Both were solidly anti-Russian.
Aberdeen would never side with the Tsar,
But what was his plan? This may sound bizarre:
For all his experience, no one knew.
His critics complained he hadn't a clue.

Russia piles on the pressure

In response to France's apparent '*coup*' –
Her despatch of the warship *Charlemagne*
To the Dardanelles, a move, in the main,
Calculated at best to stir the pot –
Nicholas determined to stop the rot
(Or did he?) by sending Prince Menshikov
To press his demands. The Turks were browned off,
Most royally, by the Prince. A lightweight,
And a joker, he told the Sultan straight:
Agree to Russia's unbridled right
Over her Christian 'subjects' – or fight.

Menshikov clearly overplayed his hand.
There were few who could fail to understand
Why the Sultan sent him packing. Yet still
Aberdeen held out hope, for good or ill,
That war could be averted. Nonetheless,
It was mad to ignore Turkey's weakness.
Britain could never stand idly by
While Russia threatened force; which is why
Six warships (on the 30th of May,
'53) set sail for Besika Bay, **1853**
By order of the British Cabinet.

Russia had not declared war, not yet,
But was poised to invade Moldavia
And Wallachia (now Romania),

Rhyming History

The Danube 'principalities', so-called.
Aberdeen and his colleagues were appalled,
Including the cautious Clarendon,
Successor to John Russell. Palmerston,
The wretch, was positively delighted.
The press were also highly excited:
Besika Bay was only a stone's throw
From the Dardanelles. Their readers should know
That the Sultan's European allies
Were ready, should the Tsar spring a surprise
And attack the Turks. In early July,
Britain's hopes for peace were blown sky high
When Nicholas's forces occupied
The said principalities. Folly? Pride?
Call it what you will, this was suicide.

The Vienna Note

The Foreign Secretary was aghast:
"The Rubicon," wrote Clarendon, "is passed."
Palmerston argued (ever divisive)
That Aberdeen should be more decisive.

Yet the PM refused to give up hope.
If Nicholas was allowed enough rope…
Who knew? On the 31st of July,
The 'Vienna Note' (it was worth a try)
Was signed by France, Britain and Russia,
After peace talks (convened by Austria,
A signatory too) determined thus:
The Russians would withdraw, without fuss,
From Turkish occupied territories –
Namely the Danube principalities –
If (but only if) the Sultan agreed
As follows. Regardless of pressing need,
He would never change, amend or review
Existing rules or customs, old or new,

The Early Victorians

Affecting his Christian subjects. No,
Such laws were to depend on the say-so
Of Russia and France, a severe blow
To Abd-el Medjid and a clear veto
Over Turkish internal policy.

The parties had behaved dishonestly.
The Sultan himself was not consulted!
Small wonder a new crisis resulted.

The Turkish ultimatum

Turkey delivered an ultimatum
To Russia. The moment had now come.
Unless, within the space of a fortnight,
Nicholas's forces gave up the fight
In the principalities, it was war.
This move Clarendon could only deplore.
"The beastly Turks," he announced with feeling,
"Have declared war." All Europe was reeling.

Britain's naval squadron was standing by.
The Turks stuck to their guns, one in the eye
For Tsar Nicholas. The Sultan was well aware
That France and Britain were sure to be there,
Should the need arise. He was unafraid,
Knowing the allies would come to his aid.

Aberdeen's habit was to sit and brood.
Wee Johnny Russell, in bellicose mood,
Was all for sending the Royal Navy
Into the Black Sea immediately,
The Baltic to boot. The old curmudgeon
Was even supported by Clarendon.
Should the pesky Russians dare to attack,
Our fleet would be ready to drive them back.

Aberdeen fought a rearguard action
Against the hawks. Sheer stupefaction
He felt, a sort of incredulity,
Faced with such dangerous tomfoolery.
The poor fellow felt it most cruelly.

The hawks prevail

The PM sought to keep the peace, but failed.
The bellicose majority prevailed.
Russell and Palmerston both had their say,
And along with Clarendon won the day.
Aberdeen's strategy of 'wait and see'
Was discredited. The Royal Navy
Would be despatched in force to the Black Sea,
Should Russia open hostilities.
This was the most reckless of policies.

Skirmishes had already taken place
In the Caucasus, both sides losing face,
A victory here, the odd defeat there,
But not in the Black Sea. They wouldn't dare...
Or would they? Aberdeen was in despair.
Any day now open war could break out.
The risk was real, he hadn't a doubt.

The Russian attack on Sinope

On the northern coastal tip of Turkey,
On the southernmost shore of the Black Sea,
Lay the small harbour town of Sinope.
Turkish ships had been spotted sheltering
In the port. Now this was the very thing
The Russians feared: a hostile presence
In the Black Sea. To the Turks it made sense.
Their ships were there to supply their armies
In the occupied principalities

And the Caucasus. To the Tsar this smacked
Of treachery: he resented the fact
That the Turks were sailing around, scot free,
In and out of their ports on the Black Sea,
Indulged and encouraged, apparently,
By the British. This was grossly unfair.
The canny old Turks were fully aware
That Aberdeen opposed all such moves. Well,
It made little difference, truth to tell.

With a force from their Black Sea naval base,
Sebastopol, the Russians played their ace.
Their fleet launched a ferocious attack
On the Turks. There was no holding them back.
November the 30th was the date
When the port of Sinope met its fate.

Russia's devastating fire-power
Destroyed the Turks in under an hour,
Their ships, their transports, along with their crews –
A hideous toll, whatever your views.
Soon the whole of Sinope was alight:
According to rumour, it burned all night.
4,000 were killed in the inferno,
Many more wounded. As disasters go,
One of the worst in Turkish history.

It was hailed as a famous victory
By the Tsar. The shore of the Black Sea
Was littered with corpses. Sinope
Would long linger in the memory.

The press in Britain enjoyed a field day.
The Times, in its wisdom, had this to say:
Russia's "consummate hypocrisy"
In attempting to "convert the Black Sea"
Into what it called "a Russian lake"
Must now be challenged. No more give and take.
This was a massacre, for Heaven's sake,

The Early Victorians

The most "frightful carnage". What this ignores,
Of course, is that the Russians had cause,
Legitimate cause, to launch their assault.
The whole thing, sadly, was the Sultan's fault.

For the Turks, remember, just weeks before,
Had moved the goalposts by declaring war.
It was they who opened hostilities.
This disturbing truth, of all ironies,
Put the Tsar in the right. So I ask you,
What were the Russians supposed to do,
When a Turkish flotilla, in full view,
Lay open to attack, packed with supplies,
And men to boot? Why, take it by surprise!

War fever in Britain

In London, though, the pack was in full cry.
Prince Albert, they said, was a Russian spy,
His kinship to the Tsar the reason why.
Palmerston, the hero of the hour,
Resigned. Albert was off to the Tower,
So rumour ran, with Aberdeen in tow,
Traitors both! This dispiriting sideshow
Demonstrated the lengths that folk would go
To press their government into action.
Russell and Clarendon, the war faction,
Led the way. Aberdeen was horrified
At the bitter outcry. To stem the tide?
Impossible. "In a case of this kind,"
He observed (few others were of like mind),
"I dread public support." The die was cast.

The Royal Navy squadron, at long last,
Prepared to sail to Constantinople.
Imagine anything quite so noble:

To move unchallenged into the Black Sea
To protect the threatened Turks. Sinope
Had been a flashpoint. Yet nobody knew
Just what our chaps were expected to do,
Once they had driven the enemy fleet
Back to Sebastopol. Clarendon, upbeat
And ever optimistic, nonetheless
(As an honest bloke) was forced to confess
That he hadn't a clue what to do next.

The British public were far from perplexed.
The Tsar should be given a bloody nose.
The war must be fought, and fought to a close,
To put the Russian Bear in his place.
There was no wider plan. A perfect disgrace.

The drift towards war

The first three months of 1854   **1854**
Saw Britain slowly "drifting towards war" –
These were Lord Derby's words. Never before
Had British policy been so muddled.
Aberdeen was confused and befuddled.
In the second week of January,
The Royal Navy entered the Black Sea.
On the 28th of February,
An advance detachment of the Army
Set sail for the East. It was now too late
To turn back and leave the Turks to their fate.

The Tsar refused to pull out his armies
From the occupied principalities.
A Franco-British ultimatum passed
For withdrawal. So it was war at last.
March the 28th was the fateful date.
Palmerston and his cronies couldn't wait,

The Early Victorians

Though Clarendon warned he was not quite sure
How to force the Russians to withdraw
From the disputed territories, or,
Come to that, how the allies could defend
Constantinople! Where would it all end?

Protection of Turkish interests
Was one thing. This most bitter of contests
Was sure, however, to mean more than that.
This was no simple war of tit-for-tat.
The one and only certain guarantee
Of the Navy's command of the Black Sea
Was to take the fight to the enemy.
Britain's First Lord of the Admiralty,
Sir James Graham, told Clarendon, for free,
That he could foresee no security
"For the peace of Europe" (or anywhere)
Unless we draw "the eye-tooth of the Bear" –
Viz. Sebastopol. Clarendon agreed.

But how was such an attack to proceed?
Sebastopol was strongly fortified.
To seize the naval base from the land side,
To the north, would need massive resources –
Overwhelming fire-power, horses,
Ammunition and men. From the sea,
To the south? An impossibility.
All the experts in the military
Were of one mind. They were forced to agree:
Sebastopol was impregnable,
A naval assault far from sensible.

The base remained a target nonetheless.
Warned of the slender chances of success,
The likes of Clarendon could not care less.
They never gave defeat a second thought.
Armchair politics: a dangerous sport.

Rhyming History

The state of the armed forces

The siege of Sebastopol, for good or ill,
Would take a modicum of martial skill
Unique in modern times. No major war
Had been fought for forty years. Furthermore,
Britain's Army was rotten to the core.
Cuts in expenditure had been severe,
Down from forty-three million a year
To just nine and a half, a heavy blow.
Were numbers sustainable? Sadly, no.
Recruitment was low, desertion rife
And discipline poor, you can bet your life.

Drunkenness was the order of the day.
The officer class, I'm sorry to say,
Were a joke, though in a different way.
Few had any experience of war.
They entered the Army through the back door,
Purchasing their commissions. It's true.
Few found anything constructive to do,
Beyond designing their own battle dress.
The Army was in one heck of a mess.

The Royal Navy, I have to confess,
Was not much better, a motley crew –
Low on experience, elderly too,
Men on whom the nation pinned its hopes.
"There is hardly a man who knows the ropes,"
Complained Sir Charles Napier in despair.

Yet there was optimism in the air.
The 1st Coldstream Guards left Trafalgar Square,
For Waterloo Station, to wild cheers.
Their fellow foot guards, the 3rd Grenadiers,
Were mobbed on the bridge. The Scots Fusiliers
Were dubbed by Queen Victoria, one hears,

"Our beautiful guards". The case was made:
The Turkish war was a moral crusade!

Lord Raglan

At Waterloo, Wellington's right hand man
Had been FitzRoy Somerset. Lord Raglan,
As he became, was now aged sixty-five,
Better fitted than any man alive
To be the Army's Commander-in-Chief.
This, at least, was the popular belief.

In the Crimea Raglan came to grief,
Shouldering the blame for incompetence,
Fatal lack of planning, and negligence
On a grand scale. Yet his honest good sense,
And courage, shone through. He made no pretence,
Though no great tactician, of the risk
Of laying siege to Sebastopol. Brisk,

But courteous, Raglan had wit and charm.
Surgeons had to amputate his right arm,
Without anaesthetic, at Waterloo.
He called for it back! What else could he do?
On his hand he had been wearing a ring
From his beloved wife. His suffering,
Against such a loss, counted for nothing.

On the field of battle his bravery
Was legendary. Yet, as we shall see,
Raglan was no leader. Hardworking, true,
His experience gained at Waterloo
Was sadly not enough. He showed respect
For the French (no less than you would expect)
And spoke the language with fluency,
Though often calling them "the enemy".
Old memories of past campaigns, you see…
We shall follow his progress as we go,
But was he a second Wellington? No.

Forward from Constantinople

So it was that Raglan went off to war.
His Lordship's first duty was to secure
The safety of Constantinople. Well,
This gave him little trouble, truth to tell.
When Raglan's men arrived at Scutari,
In April, a stone's throw from the Black Sea,
News filtered through of Turkish successes
On the Danube. Russian excesses
In the occupied principalities
Had been curbed. The enemy, by degrees,
Had melted away and now proved no threat
To Constantinople – at least, not yet.

From Scutari therefore, in early June,
Raglan, surfing this wave of good fortune,

Moved north to Varna, on the Black Sea coast,
Three hundred miles distant. What mattered most
Was to back our brave Turkish allies
By taking the Russians by surprise,
Should they head for northern Bulgaria.
In this rugged, mountainous area
Their exhausted troops would stand little chance.

Britain's French allies

Raglan's forces joined up with those of France
And this is where it started to go wrong.
There had been some friction, all along,
Between the French Commander, Saint-Arnaud,
A bristling, prickly so-and-so,
And the modest, easy-going Raglan.
There was no common strategy or plan.
For example, on the 18th of May,
The Turks, French and British all had their say
In a new agreement to hold at bay
The Russians in the lower Danube.

Saint-Arnaud then claimed to have made a boob
And back-tracked on the decision made.
He balked at moving to Varna, afraid,
He said, that the French were not yet ready
To come to the aid of the Turks. Steady,
Courageous, and a man of his word,
To his lasting credit Raglan demurred.
He would press ahead with the allied plan.

Hats off to his Lordship! A complex man,
Saint-Arnaud then changed his tactics again.
The French sailed to Varna, there to remain
Through a sweltering summer. Boredom, heat
And sickness were the enemies to beat.

Rhyming History

A terrible start

In early April, at Gallipoli,
Raglan's advance troops had suffered badly
From hunger and cold. They waited for days –
The scandal never ceases to amaze –
For the most basic supplies to arrive:
Food, bedding, tents... How were they to survive?

Sadly, many failed to make it. Disease
Was already rampant. "The rats! The fleas!"
Wrote Fanny Duberly, whose diaries
Tell a bleak story. This of Scutari,
Another treat in store for the Army:
"Filthy beggars hovering everywhere,"
She recorded in disgust and despair,
"Refuse of every description."

This (no surprise) was a prescription
For death and disease. Cholera had struck,
Already, in Malta. It took some pluck
To endure the utter squalor and stench,
Given the knowledge that the pesky French
Were better supplied with medicines, tents
And regular meals. This caused much offence.
Raglan suffered from awful diarrhoea,
The poor soul. Welcome to the Crimea!

One arrival caused a comic hiccup.
When the 93rd Highlanders pitched up,
In their kilts, the good folk of Scutari
Were lost for words. For they could only be,
These hairy laddies, his Lordship's harem,
Hussies of whom the Turks could only dream.

Back to Varna. Some sixty miles away,
At Silistria, to the Tsar's dismay,

The Early Victorians

His army faltered and drifted away.
The Turks had dug in and they won the day.

Where did the wretched Russians go wrong?
It's hard to fathom. Fifty thousand-strong,
They threw in the towel. It now appeared,
To some, that the threat all Europe had feared
Had passed – *viz.* a Russian invasion.

Now this was the obvious occasion
For a radical rethink by the allies.
Regrettably, folk at home thought otherwise.
There was no desire to give up the fight.
Silistria fed the public appetite
For giving Russia a bloody nose,
And this, it was only fair to suppose,
Must mean an attack on Sebastopol.

Rhyming History

Disease, death and disaster

The allies, after all, were on a roll –
Or were they? Far from it, to be honest.
For Varna provided a deadly twist.
Cholera was rampant, out of control.
10,000 British perished, a huge toll,
And 7,000 French. The searing heat,
The drink, and with nothing decent to eat,
Left all but the fittest dead on their feet.
Provisions were still in short supply –
Few tents, no blankets… no idea why.

To add to the allies' common malaise,
On the 10th of August a massive blaze
Destroyed their stores: thousands of pairs of shoes,
Reserves of rations, even their booze.

William Russell

All these disasters were soon in the news,
Thanks to one William Howard Russell,
Of *The Times*. Flexing his paper's muscle
As an early foreign correspondent,
He was quick to record the discontent
Of the troops and the horrors of the war.
People had never read the like before.
He wrote of men "covered with swarms of flies"
Lying "drunk in the kennels". No surprise,
Therefore, that when his reports filtered through
The readership at home turned the air blue
With contempt and disgust. Poor Aberdeen,
His popularity nose-dived. The Queen
Was spared the gruesome details – too graphic,
For sure. With a keen eye for the tragic,
Russell never glossed over the slaughter:
"Dead bodies bobbed about in the water,

The Early Victorians

"All buoyant, bolt upright and hideous
"In the sun." The over-fastidious
Could only hope that Russell falsified
His dispatches. Others were horrified.
The reports were no exaggeration.
They spoke the truth and they shamed the nation.

Target: Sebastopol

Yet in spite of Russell the public mood
Was for war. The government's attitude,
If anything, had hardened: Clarendon,
Russell (not William, the other one),
Newcastle and the dreaded Palmerston,
All pressed for an immediate assault
On Sebastopol. The hawks were at fault,
And Aberdeen knew it. So did Raglan,
To be fair. But the measure of the man
Was such that he had not the slightest doubt
That orders were there to be carried out.

Amazingly, nobody seemed quite sure
Of Russian numbers. To go to war,
Lacking such knowledge, was pure lunacy.
Franco-British strength, numerically,
Was 30,000 (approximately)
For the French, and for the British (roughly)
26,000. The Turks had no more
Than 6,000, making a total score
Of 62,000. To overawe
The mighty Russians, was this enough?
Hardly. The Tsar was made of sterner stuff.
How many men could he muster? The truth,
We now know, was some 80,000. Strewth!

But British intelligence, at a guess
(A pitiful shower), hazarded less:

Just 45,000 – no more, they said.
The Commander-in-Chief, take it as read,
Had no statistics to offer at all,
Though the odds, he feared, were too close to call.

Few maps, no strategy…

Raglan had few maps of any value.
A war council, to decide what to do,
Was convened on the 18th of July.
The key issue at stake was how (not why)
The siege of Sebastopol should proceed.
Yet apart from a vague will to succeed,
There was precious little strategy.
The Navy, in command of the Black Sea,
Would attack from the south, while the Army
Would close in from the north, on the land side.
So far, so good… but this was suicide,
And Raglan, in his bones, surely knew it.
Winter was approaching. If he blew it,
He was finished; but he would take his chance.

The order had been given to advance.
So off went Britain, arm in arm with France,
To face the Russians at Sebastopol.
What folly. The siege took a terrible toll.
"Hurrah for the Crimea!" – that was the cry.
"We are off tomorrow!" – though no one knew why.
"Sebastopol falls in a week, no more!"
Saint-Arnaud had his doubts, but this he swore:
The French would return covered in glory.
Home before Christmas! The same old story.

The weather was the particular fear
Of Sir John Burgoyne, the Chief Engineer.
He dreaded the winter with good reason.
To his mind the lateness of the season

Rendered this a "desperate enterprise".
His pessimism was hard to disguise.
Already it was nearly September.
Sir John was aware that by November
Snow would lie thick on the ground. He despaired.
The Army was hopelessly ill-prepared –
No winter clothes or equipment. Who cared?
Not the politicians, that's for sure,
Nor the public at large, thirsty for war.

Landing at Kalamita

The allies landed their troops in September –
Just weeks before winter set in, remember –
At the aptly named Kalamita Bay,
A stretch of shore some thirty miles away
From Sebastopol. It is fair to say
That Raglan was fortunate in one thing.
The Russians had no earthly inkling
That his forces were planning a landing.
Under the feeble command (now don't scoff)
Of that comedian, Prince Menshikov,
They adopted a craven policy,
A forlorn strategy, of 'wait and see'.
They could scarcely believe, take it from me,
That the allies would be so foolhardy
As to hazard a major offensive.

So Menshikov stayed on the defensive.
Outnumbered, he reckoned, in men, horses,
Guns, equipment and other resources,
He preferred to concentrate his forces
On the defence of Sebastopol. So,
Although time was tight and progress was slow,
Saint-Arnaud and Raglan landed their men
Without fear of attack. What happened then?

Rhyming History

Confusion! I don't wish to be rude,
But the British disembarked short of food
And lacking cover. A perfect disgrace.
They suffered embarrassing loss of face
When they saw that the French, the first ashore,
Were provided with food and tents galore.
The preparations for a short war
Were wholly inadequate. Furthermore,
There was no sign of hospital transport.
Ambulance wagons had been left in port,
At Varna. When the dread cholera struck,
Its pitiful victims were out of luck,
Some of them so sick they could barely move.
They were left to suffer. What did this prove?
Answer: no one knew what they had started.
Raglan was a kindly man, good-hearted,
Conscientious and sympathetic.
As a planner, however? Pathetic.

Picture this: after the helter-skelter
Of the landings, a night without shelter.
The heavens opened and the rain set in.
The poor men, hungry and soaked to the skin,
Huddled under their coats as best they could.
They tried to make fires out of driftwood,
A desperate and dispiriting task.
How were these sad fellows, I hear you ask,
To do battle? I have no idea,
But freshly arrived in the Crimea
They determined to make the best of it.

The next day the weather improved a bit.
The sun came out. They could cook up some food.
By all accounts in belligerent mood,
Their colours flying high, the troops set out
On the road to Sebastopol. A rout?
An assured success, no shadow of doubt.

The first battle

The River Alma lay across their way.
Turning their backs on Kalamita Bay,
It did not take them long to realise
That Menshikov planned to spring a surprise
At the Alma. The British had their spies.
They were therefore not slow to understand
That the Prince must draw a line in the sand
If he wanted to halt enemy progress
Towards Sebastopol. I have to confess
That he rose to the challenge. Anything less,
And he might just as well have opened wide
The city gate. Military suicide.

This was the first pitched battle of the war.
Few of the men had seen action before.

Rhyming History

Warfare was the great unknown. Defeat
Was unthinkable. In the searing heat,
The fighting lasted over three hours,
Four of the great European powers
Locked in mortal combat. A lofty ridge,
South of the river, gave the advantage
To the Russians. The French scaled the heights
Under heavy fire. You'd think, by rights,
The Russians should have driven the French back.

But Menshikov found himself under attack
On a number of fronts. He dithered, the fool,
While Raglan maintained his customary cool.
The outcome, however, was too close to call,
With the Turks, we're told, doing nothing at all.

A victory of sorts

Raglan's plans were poorly co-ordinated,
With early hopes of a breakthrough frustrated.
The infantry, though, in the thick of the fray,
Bayonets at the ready, carried the day.
The Russians fled in complete disarray.

No clear record of casualties survives,
But the Alma claimed over 5,000 lives,
Most of them Russian. How much does this tell
Of the true horror, the veritable hell
Of the slaughter? Very little, in my view.
William Howard Russell, over to you.
Few could conceive "the relics of a great fight",
The grass "slippy with blood", a terrible sight.
The stench of the battlefield he describes well,
Too well: "a sickening, sour, foetid smell".

What next? The Russian forces had fled,
No time to tend to their wounded. Instead,

The Early Victorians

They straggled away to await, they feared,
An allied onslaught. It never appeared.
Raglan wanted to pursue Menshikov.
The Light Brigade were thoroughly hacked off
When they received no order to do so.
Raglan sought the support of Saint-Arnaud
To follow up their recent victory,
Take Sebastopol and make history.
Saint-Arnaud, sadly, was a dying man.
He refused to countenance Raglan's plan.
His troops were exhausted. They needed rest.

Frustrated, Raglan did his level best
To persuade the French Commander-in-Chief
To change his tactics, firm in the belief
That to storm Sebastopol, unopposed,
Was a gift. It can only be supposed
That the noble Raglan was disinclined
To offend the French. His Lordship, you'll find,
Was far too obliging for his own good.
The Russians must have been touching wood.
Lucky or what? The allies were barmy
Not to give chase. The Russian army
In the Crimea, what was left of it,
Was sick at heart and less than fighting fit.

The allies hung around for a few days
On the Alma. They buried (beyond praise)
Swathes of Russian dead. Balaklava
Was the next port of call. Some palaver
Was had between Raglan and Saint-Arnaud.
Largely again on the latter's say-so,
They agreed that this would prove a sound base
For the British, a well-appointed place
To prepare for their assault, in due course,
On Sebastopol. The main allied force
Would consolidate their strength and take stock.

Rhyming History

A new French Commander

The French then suffered a sobering shock.
Saint-Arnaud resigned and went home to die,
Replaced by Canrobert, goodness knows why.
The British and French were alike appalled –
'Robert Can't' the fellow came to be called.
Saint-Arnaud was suffering, the poor man,
From cancer. Raglan was hardly a fan,
But after he left the trouble began.

Russian reinforcements

Raglan learned from naval intelligence
That massive resources for the defence
Of Sebastopol had lately arrived.
Whether the Russians could have survived,
Had the allies launched an early assault,
Was now a moot point. Were the French at fault?
Who knows? Besides, an attack from the north
Had become extremely risky. Henceforth,
The plan was to approach from the south-east.
This was one of the benefits, at least,
Of Balaklava. Strong lines of supply
Were another boon. Easy on the eye,
It was a pretty little spot to boot.
On several grounds it was sure to suit.

Dream on. The Tsar was painfully aware
That there was precious little time to spare
Before the allies would be at the gate
Of Sebastopol. They'd be mad to wait
Until the spring, with winter in prospect.
He was certainly right in that respect.
Allied preparations had begun
For an autumn siege. It would not be fun,
But Raglan knew that it had to be done.

The Early Victorians

The attack on Balaklava

The Russians considered otherwise.
They would take the enemy by surprise
By pre-empting the siege. Something had to give.
The Russians seized the initiative
By launching a sudden attack, at dawn,
On Balaklava. Battle lines were drawn
As Raglan, to defend his power base,
Hastily put his cavalry in place.
Many of his men were deployed elsewhere,
But Raglan was never one to despair.
He summoned reinforcements, well aware
That Russia's General Liprandi
Had some 25,000 infantry
And thirty-four squadrons of cavalry,
Supported by heavy artillery,
At his command. A formidable force.

Their early surprise arrival, of course,
Gave the Russians a huge advantage.
The Turks had the dubious privilege
Of bearing the brunt of their first attack.
The Ottoman forces were driven back,
Overwhelmed by Liprandi's cavalry.
The Turks showed astonishing bravery,
In this, their most courageous of stands.

Some British naval guns, one understands,
Were seized by the enemy. Shame indeed.
Balaklava, in its hour of need,
Now lay wide open to the enemy.
Out of sight, however, of the cavalry,
Were waiting Sir Colin Campbell's infantry,
The famed 93rd Highlanders. Without fear,
They held their ground. Sir Colin's words were clear.
"Remember, there is no escape from here,"

Rhyming History

He told his men. "You must die where you stand."
These indomitable sons of Scotland
Opened fire upon the enemy.
Russell describes a "thundering volley".

The Russians turned tail, in disarray.
The "thin red line" is recalled, to this day,
In Tennyson's verse – a bit of a cheek,
Given Russell's earlier "thin red streak,
"Topped with a line of steel". Now on parade
Came the British so-called 'Heavy Brigade'.
They were ordered to move up in support,
To see off the Russians. How they fought!
Riding uphill, at no more than a trot,
They gave the Russians as good as they got.
Outnumbered 800 to 3,000,
The Heavies surged forward. They gave no ground.
The enemy were thunderstruck. Spellbound,
Helpless and desperate, they quitted the fray.

Yet this was to be Raglan's darkest day.
He sought to recover the captured guns.
The Heavy and Light Brigades were the ones
Ordered to achieve this great objective.
Lord Lucan was at first unresponsive
To the order. This was hard to forgive.

Commander of the British cavalry,
Lucan was to advance immediately,
With expected support from the infantry,
And make use of "any opportunity"
To recapture the guns. Lucan perceived
This command (if he is to be believed)
To mean that he was only to advance
Together with the infantry. Fat chance.
The back-up forces were far from ready.
Lord Lucan, lacklustre and unsteady,

The Early Victorians

Stood his men at ease. Through his field glasses,
Raglan saw his troops, the silly asses,
Relaxing in the sun. All Lucan's fault!

He gave renewed orders for an assault:
"Lord Raglan wishes the cavalry"
(This *verbatim*) "to advance rapidly
"To the front, follow the enemy
"And try to prevent the enemy
"Carrying away the guns." Clear, you see.
He went on: "Troop Horse Artillery
"May accompany. French cavalry
"Is on your left. Immediate." Airey,
Lord Raglan's dependable ADC,
Made a rare mistake. Raglan's scribbled note,
Which, it has to be said, his Lordship wrote
In the heat of the moment, Airey passed
To Captain Nolan. We should stand aghast
At the subsequent grim chain of events.

Nolan was a man of limited sense,
Hot-headed and reckless to a degree.
The fool was also Airey's ADC.
Raglan approved the choice of this wild man
To deliver his note. "Tell Lord Lucan"
(Raglan's parting words) "the cavalry
"Is to attack immediately."
It's worth noting in passing that Nolan
Was dismissive not only of Lucan,
But deeply contemptuous of Raglan.

So this is how the fiasco began.
Lucan could not see the guns referred to.
Raglan, of course, imagined Lucan knew.
He didn't. "Attack, sir?" he asked Nolan,
To whom the war was just a bit of fun,

Rhyming History

"Attack what? What guns, sir?" It seems to me
That this was fair. All poor Lucan could see
Was a heavy Russian battery
At the far end of an exposed valley.
Nolan gestured: "There is your enemy!"
Raglan's orders "to advance rapidly"
Were clear from the note. What was he to do?

The Light Brigade

Well, maybe the Earl of Cardigan knew,
A most surly character, to be sure,
And Lucan's detested brother-in-law.
Cardigan commanded the Light Brigade,
One of the worst appointments ever made
In the history of British warfare.
His officers were reduced to despair.
According to one, the Earl was a brute,
A dull fool, with "as much brains as my boot".

He drilled his regiment three times a day,
Dressed (at his expense) in finest array –
Short blue jackets, tight trousers in cherry,
Parading through Windsor, Londonderry
And Brighton. Ten thousand a year he spent,
His men admired wherever they went –
The 'Cherry Bums', as they came to be called.
His officers, though, were duly appalled
By his red-hot temper. One of life's cranks,
A beast to boot, he was loathed in the ranks.
A martinet, floggings were commonplace.
The Earl, in short, was a proper disgrace.

Yet he never showed the slightest remorse.
He purchased his commission, of course –
A cool forty thousand pounds it cost him.
For Cardigan was rich as well as dim.

The Early Victorians

His extravagant purchase cost him dear,
And many a soldier too, I fear.
At Balaklava he slept on his yacht
In warmth and comfort, the drunken old sot,
While his men lay out in the cold night air,
Exposed to the moon. Did Cardigan care?
Not a jot. Whoever said life was fair?

The brothers-in-law were at daggers drawn.
Greater enemies had never been born.
The ghastly Earl was a figure of scorn
To the loathsome Lucan. They barely spoke.
Which was the more disagreeable bloke?
By a whisker, Cardigan gets my vote.

So when Lucan received the dreaded note,
He delivered the order in person,
Without discussing it, to Cardigan.
Did either man fully understand it?
Raglan's command had been "immediate",
But Cardigan had strong reservations.
One of the Earl's main considerations
Were the lines of Russian artillery,
And riflemen, that he could plainly see
On every side, flanking the valley.
Despite their mutual antipathy,
The brothers-in-law were forced to agree.
Lord Raglan's orders must be carried out.

Beyond the faintest shadow of a doubt,
Cardigan displayed great courage that day.
The hapless Lucan, I regret to say,
Showed nothing of the kind. "Take it away!"
Cried Captain Nolan, as he stormed forward,
Leading the charge and brandishing his sword.
This madcap officer, the first to die,
Hit the ground with an agonising cry.

Rhyming History

They never stood a chance, the Light Brigade.
Onward they charged! Cardigan, undismayed,
Led his men, against overwhelming odds,
Through the so-called 'Valley of Death'. Ye gods!
Under heavy fire the men surged on,
Through swirling smoke as black as Acheron.
A mile and a half they rode, with lances
And sabres. Each took a thousand chances.

The men who made it, astonishingly,
To the end of that infernal valley,
Engaged the massed Russian cavalry
In bloody battle. Then they turned around
And rode back over the very same ground
Whence they had come, now littered with the dead,
The dying and the wounded. It was said,
With pride, that no man surrendered. Instead,
They lived to be heroes of history.
Who was to blame remains a mystery.

The Early Victorians

There were too many fingers in the pie.
Raglan held Lucan responsible. Why?

Well, he clearly failed to challenge Nolan,
Who brought the order direct from Raglan.
Nor did he deign to answer Cardigan
When he aired his doubts. Bitterly pursued,
Lucan and Cardigan's family feud
Was to some degree to blame for the mess.
Then again, Nolan's conduct was reckless,
Wilful and wild. It was a crying shame
That he fell, but he was also to blame.

Cardigan was disgusted and angry
When Raglan had the gross effrontery
To take him to task for leading the charge.
The haughty Earl replied that, by and large,
He would rather expect to have been praised
For following orders. Eyebrows were raised.
Was this any way to speak to Raglan?

He hardly cared. The buck stopped with Lucan.
Raglan had to agree. The case was made.
In few words – "You have lost the Light Brigade" –
His Lordship vented his utter disgust
On Lucan. Now accept that if you must,
But I am not prepared to exculpate
Raglan himself. Before it was too late,
He should at least have paused to clarify
His order. Lucan was forced to comply
With his will, as he interpreted it,
And as he and his brother-in-law saw fit.

Why did Lucan's 'Heavies' fail to follow
The Light Brigade? Excuses look hollow.
Did he lose his nerve? If we only knew.
Danger and cowardice, a potent brew.

Rhyming History

The aftermath

The dead numbered one hundred and seven,
From a total force, merciful Heaven,
Of six hundred and seventy. Tennyson
Calls them "the six hundred". Poetic licence.
If you are a poet, it sometimes makes sense
To round down the numbers. But this you should know:
Each and every man was a true hero
Who fell that day. Some one hundred and sixty
Were sorely wounded, their place in history
Assured. And remember, when counting the cost,
The four hundred horses that were also lost.

Nolan's bravado, his 'devil-may-care',
And Cardigan's too, I am well aware,
Fell foul of the rules. A deadly affair.
"C'est magnifique, mais ce n'est pas la guerre,"
Opined Marshal Bosquet. I call that fair.

Tennyson tells us that "someone had blundered",
As into the valley "rode the six hundred".
They charged regardless, "while all the world wondered",
As cannons on all sides "volleyed and thundered".
The poem will bring a tear to your eye.
It cuts to the heart. Why, I hear you cry,
Should such a sacrifice ever be made?
Well, that's the way of the world, I'm afraid.

The outcome of the battle? A stalemate!
Balaklava itself, at any rate,
Remained in British hands. The enemy,
However, hailed it as a victory.
They now controlled the heights around the town.
The Brits would gradually be ground down,
Cut off from the French and starved of supplies.

The Early Victorians

The approach of winter

Winter lay ahead. It's no surprise
That spirits were low. All was not lost,
But men reported a touch of frost,
An ominous sign, that awful night.
The future was looking far from bright.

October the 25th was the date
When those heroes of legend met their fate.
November was far too late in the year
To lay siege to Sebastopol, I fear,
With any prospect of total success.
Some 35,000 troops, nonetheless,
Had dug themselves in around the city.
Their state of morale though, more's the pity,
Was poor. This was well known to Raglan.

Inkerman

North of Balaklava, Mount Inkerman
Offered a lifeline, a strategic spot
From which to take a determined pot shot
At the enemy. It lay to the east
Of Sebastopol. At the very least,
British marksmen could keep an eagle eye
On the chief Russian line of supply
From the outside world to Sebastopol –
Namely, the main road from Simferopol.
By the same token, the Russians knew
There was one sure thing that they had to do:
Dislodge the pesky Brits from Inkerman.
A sudden surprise attack was the plan.

The date set was the 5th of November,
Less than a fortnight, you may remember,

Rhyming History

After Balaklava. Much was at stake.
Menshikov knew that it was make or break,
But was guilty of one fatal mistake:
Overconfidence. The allies, it's true,
Were outnumbered, but this was nothing new.
He imagined that all he had to do
Was give the order – mad, but there you are.
The Prince was seriously under par,
A washout. He was terrified, in fact,
Of battle! Surely he should have been sacked
After the Alma. As Commander-in-Chief,
His utter incompetence defied belief.

When the attack on Inkerman began,
Menshikov, sadly, had no battle plan –
No maps, no leadership, no strategy.
At six a.m. the Russian infantry
Took the British position by storm.
Caught on the hop, Lord Raglan, true to form,
Kept his cool. His infantry were well-drilled,
And his officers spirited, strong-willed,
Courageous and true. Nevertheless,
The Battle of Inkerman was a mess –
The most desperate hand-to-hand fighting,
Every man for himself. Exciting?
Hardly. The tide of battle ebbed and flowed,
Bloody and terrible. Pity be blowed.
Kill or be killed. Massacred like cattle,
Cut down in swathes, 'a soldier's battle' –
That is how history refers to it.
'A bloodbath' would be far more apposite.

For nine hellish hours the battle raged,
British and Russians, fiercely engaged.
Bayonets were used to deadly effect,
The death toll as high as you would expect.

Some five hundred and ninety-seven died,
With thousands wounded, on the British side.
Over 10,000 Russians breathed their last,
Or suffered wounds. Survivors stood aghast:
"*Quel abattoir!*" – Marshal Bosquet again.
The French contingent lost just thirteen men,
Though many more bore shocking injuries.

Inkerman was heralded, if you please,
As a triumph. The Queen honoured the dead,
The battle won "by their blood freely shed".
"Noble and successful" was the struggle.

The sad truth was, the war was a muddle.
The Army was overstretched, underfed
And ill-equipped. To glorify the dead –
Fine. But what the poor troops wanted instead
Were boots, warm clothing and medical care,
Tents and nourishment. Men were in despair.

Taking stock of the war

Raglan informed the British government
That of 30,000 men lately sent
To the Crimea, 6,000 had died.
Of those lucky enough to have survived,
8,000 had been wounded, or were sick
Of the cholera. They needed a kick:
Aberdeen's ministers had to be quick.
Reinforcements were urgently needed.

At Inkerman the British succeeded,
Against all the odds, in winning the day.
Yet Raglan acknowledged, to his dismay,
That his men, far from being on a roll,
Were in no state to take Sebastopol.

Rhyming History

Plans for an autumn siege were a dead duck.
The allies were spent and down on their luck,
Cold, hungry and dispirited to boot.

Back home, Aberdeen didn't give a hoot.
That was the widely held view anyway.
This was quite unfair, I am bound to say.
The Prime Minister's own beloved son,
To wit, Colonel Alexander Gordon,
Had distinguished himself at Inkerman,
Escaping death "owing to the mercy
"Of God", though "my horse was shot under me".

Alex made the case for vital supplies,
Adding his voice to other plaintive cries
For reinforcements. He warned his father,
An enforced winter in Balaklava
Would probably be as good as it got.
The planned siege of Sebastopol was not
(Repeat, not) now likely to go ahead
Before the spring. The troops were poorly fed –
He would never have dared say poorly led –
Exhausted and suffering from disease.
The Crimean Army was on its knees.

General Sir George de Lacy Evans
Went further. To Lord Raglan (great Heavens)
He was bold enough to proffer advice.
Sebastopol? Too great a sacrifice!
"My Lord, save your army," he told his boss,
"And raise the siege." Raglan was at a loss.
I am sure in his heart his Lordship agreed,
But orders were orders. He had to succeed.
Even Clarendon, Foreign Secretary,
Was fearful of a "monster catastrophe".
So wrote the Earl to Lord Stratford de Redcliffe.
"God grant I may be wrong," he added. As if.

A deadly storm

Matters were yet to go from bad to worse.
The November weather gave cause to curse.
A mighty, terrifying hurricane
Blew up just ten days after Inkerman.

Tents were flattened, half the horses broke free –
Destruction as far as the eye could see.
The poor men were left drenched and shivering.

The great storm scattered and smashed up shipping
In Balaklava harbour. The worst loss
Was the steamship *Prince*. In all the chaos,
The transport vessel broke up on the rocks
And sank, with vital cargo: warm clothes, socks,
Uniforms and boots, 40,000 pairs!
This, to be sure, was the stuff of nightmares.
Six crew were saved, from a total number
Of one hundred and fifty. Small wonder

Rhyming History

That morale collapsed to an all-time low.
The tempest gave way to flurries of snow,
The first of the winter. Blizzards and sleet,
Bitter gales from the north and blistered feet...
With four months of this to look forward to,
How were the troops to survive? No one knew.

The hospital at Scutari

Cholera swept through the ranks, as we've seen.
Hospital conditions were obscene.
The only medical facility
For the British troops was at Scutari,
A long and uncomfortable journey
Of three hundred miles across the Black Sea.
Here young Florence Nightingale made her name,
The 'Lady with the Lamp' her claim to fame.

The British Military Hospital
Was in a parlous state, unspeakable –
No linen, no dressings, no clean water...
One victim of the terrible slaughter,
A rotting corpse, in a state of decay,
Was the cause of not a little dismay –
Putrid, offensive and foul as it lay
In the nurses' quarters. Without delay,
Florence set to work. The water supply
She found to be contaminated. Why?
When the lid of the tank was uncovered,
The decomposed body was discovered
Of a horse. Many men who had survived
The Alma were there when Florence arrived.

Then in mid-November, shortly after,
The sick and wounded of Balaklava,
And later from Inkerman, joined the ranks.
Some poor wretches were sparing in their thanks.

The Early Victorians

Those who lived through the terrible ordeal
Of the Black Sea passage, how did they feel?
Fearful and horrified is my best guess.

Florence was sensitive to their distress.
Writing home, after her service began,
"Not an average of three limbs per man"
Was her estimate. She wrote from the heart:
"We have four miles of beds" (where did she start?),
These no more than "eighteen inches apart".
Conditions were filthy, equipment,
Supplies and bandages non-existent.

Florence Nightingale's character

Miss Nightingale's great strength was management.
This fine woman was hard-working, forthright,
Bossy (at times) and formidably bright.
She set to with a will. She got things done,
Rallying support from everyone.
She was a "general dealer," she said,
"In socks, shirts, wooden spoons…" Take it as read,
Whatever the challenge she kept her head.
"Tin baths, operating tables, bed-pans
"And stump-pillows" – all featured in her plans,
Even "cabbages, carrots, knives and forks".
Of course Florence had funds, and money talks,
But without her amazing stamina,
She would have achieved nothing. God bless her!

She met with serious opposition.
Dr. Duncan Menzies, whose position
Was Deputy Inspector-General
At the dreaded Scutari Hospital,
Reported that the wounded and the sick
Wanted for nothing – how idiotic:
Complacency verging on the psychotic.

Twenty-four hours a day on her feet,
Florence remained resolute and upbeat.
She herself suffered from dysentery
And 'Crimea Fever'. Her empathy,
Pity and compassion, quite simply,
Made the difference. It was well known
That no one would be left to die alone.

Florence Nightingale was ever at hand,
With her team of sisters, her 'Angel Band'.

The scourge of cholera, you understand,
Was the curse of the war. Casualties
From hardship, malnourishment and disease
Were two-thirds of total fatalities –
In round numbers, 60,000 British,
100,000 French and (to finish)

300,000 Russians. I regret
I have no figures for the Turks, though I bet
That many tens of thousands of them perished
In defence of the great empire they cherished.

Mary Seacole

Another pioneering heroine,
One steeped in alternative medicine,
Was Mary Seacole. Of mixed parentage –
Her mother of Jamaican heritage
And her father a Scot – 'Mother Seacole',
As she was known, was a tough old soul.
Strong as an ox, and with sound common sense,
She had thirty years of experience
As a nurse living in the West Indies.

Cholera brought Jamaica to its knees –
32,000 cases, if you please.
The victims of this terrible disease
Mary treated with her 'home' remedies:
"Mustard plasters" on the stomach and back,
"Calomel" (for the worst kind of attack),
And "warm fomentations". Folk were blessed:
A ministering angel. What was best
She selected "from my medicine chest".
She never went anywhere without it,
And who are we to have cause to doubt it?
Mother Seacole: part doctor and part nurse –
The folk of Jamaica could have done worse.

Mary befriended the officers and men
Stationed in Jamaica. Imagine, then,
How she felt when she read of the campaign
In the Crimea, of the dreadful strain
That the troops were suffering. Some she knew.
Ma Seacole was clear what she had to do.

Rhyming History

She travelled to London to volunteer
As one of Nightingale's nurses. Oh, dear:
Mary was rebuffed at every turn.
It sadly didn't take her long to learn
That her colour was the reason for this,
A blatant case of racial prejudice.
From the Crimea Fund she also sought
A grant to travel. This too came to nought.

With the tears rolling down her cheeks, Mary stood
"In the fast-running streets". Yet all would come good,
On this she was resolved. She'd go if she could.
She was bound for the Crimea, come what may.
Ever the optimist, the very next day
She had cards printed: "THE BRITISH HOTEL" –
She knew what she wanted, which augured well –
"MRS. MARY SEACOLE, *late of Kingston*,
"*Jamaica.*" Mary was sure to get on.
To start a hotel was her fixed intent.
The Crimea beckoned – so off she went!

Upon her arrival in Scutari
She sought a bed for the night. Who are we
To pass judgement on Florence Nightingale?
Mary certainly did not. But to fail
To be offered employment was nonsense,
Given her record and experience.
"What do you want?" the Englishwoman said.
"Anything we can do for you?" A bed,
No more, she was given in the washroom –
Unfit for anyone else, I presume.

She writes, "I saw much of Miss Nightingale
"At Balaklava" – but to no avail,
I suspect, since she gives little detail.
So long as Mary Seacole knew her place,
Florence was happy. A proper disgrace.

At Balaklava, Mary's claim to fame
Was the British Hotel. To great acclaim,
She built it out of nothing: old driftwood,
Iron sheets (she used anything she could),
Even packing cases and broken doors.

The edifice opened, to wild applause,
At a final cost of eight hundred pounds.
That is quite as expensive as it sounds –
But Mary was soon turning a profit.
Just as well, since she had to live off it.

She'd run a boarding house in Kingston, too,
Along with her mother. So, nothing new.
She combined her talents. "A mess-table"
Mary provided, when she was able,

And "comfortable quarters" (the words are hers)
For "sick and convalescent officers".
She also visited the battlefield
Under heavy fire, refusing to yield.
She suffered some near misses. We shall see,
When Sebastopol fell, that it was she,
Ma Seacole, who was the first woman in.
Comfort in abundance she brought, chicken,
Bandages, lemonade, cake, medicine,
Lashings of love and (quite possibly) gin.

"A warm and successful physician,"
Is how William Russell described her.
An eccentric she was, who caused a stir,
Who "doctors and cures all manner of men" –
These the chosen words of Russell again –
"With the most extraordinary success".

It was her strength of character, no less,
That was Mother Seacole's secret. She wrote
Her memoirs (from which I've ventured to quote):
*Wonderful Adventures of Mary Seacole
In Many Lands*. Sometimes tragic, often droll,
Hers is a story you cannot pigeon-hole.
Whether serving up a chicken casserole,
Or offering succour to a dying man,
Mary was a one-off. Russell was a fan.
Who cares whether Nightingale was one or not?
Mother Seacole's case was as good as it got.

The severe winter

Winter was hideous. Death and disease
Stalked the ranks of the Army. Raglan's pleas
For reinforcements and urgent supplies
Fell on deaf ears. One letter typifies

The Early Victorians

The despair, this from Colonel Gordon –
Alex, you'll recall, was Aberdeen's son:
"Several hundred wagons" were needed,
He suggested (his calls went unheeded),
"For the conveyance of ammunition."
Even Gordon's privileged position
Counted for little. Alex deserves praise
For lambasting the scandalous delays
In sending out winter clothes. Aberdeen
Was not unsympathetic, as we've seen,
But as PM he has to take the rap.
An amiable and peace-loving chap,
He was nonetheless guilty in my book.

Aberdeen resigns

Not that his Lordship was let off the hook.
In the New Year, in late January,   **1855**
John Arthur Roebuck, a backbench MP,
Put the case for a select committee
To scrutinise the conduct of the war.
This could not have upset Aberdeen more.
Eighty-five of his allies crossed the floor
To vote in favour of Roebuck's motion.
This was carried, to shows of emotion.

Lord John Russell resigned from the government.
Here was an opportunity, Heaven-sent,
To stab his good chum the PM in the back.
Poor old Aberdeen, already on the rack,
Was cut to the quick by this act of foul play
And, to Victoria's distress and dismay,
Tendered his resignation. Aberdeen
Had long been a firm favourite of the Queen.
Their parting was tearful, a most touching scene.
So "noble and disinterested" a man
Was Aberdeen – sadly though, an also-ran.

Rhyming History

A Knight of the Garter his Lordship became.
He refused in private to shoulder the blame
For the disaster of the Crimean War.
To Mary Haddo, his fond daughter-in-law,
He recorded his feelings: like it or not,
There had been "much mismanagement on the spot…
"The public here are persuaded" (self-serving rot)
"That there has also been neglect in this country".
Government defeat "by a great majority"
Rendered it "necessary for us to resign".
So, his premiership had been perfect. Fine –
A tenable view, but certainly not mine.

This gentle man retired from public life.
The censure he suffered cut like a knife.
His conduct of the war was a disgrace,
But the Cabinet hawks had set the pace.
Russell and Palmerston, a potent brew,
The Times and public opinion too,
Had painted him into a corner. Well,
The force was unstoppable, truth to tell.
So his Lordship buckled. Poor Aberdeen.
As a young man (this we've already seen),
A British envoy in 1814,
He witnessed the terrible aftermath
Of Leipzig, a veritable bloodbath.

So in '53, against all the odds,
He sought to face down those silly old sods,
Russell (a pain in the butt), Clarendon
And, most hawkish of them all, Palmerston.
Please pardon my language. I'm divided:
Aberdeen was to blame, I've decided,
For the shameful shortcomings of the war –
Most monstrous mismanagement, to be sure –
But, unlike old 'Pam', he had no hunger
For the campaign. He was no warmonger.

The Early Victorians

He would miss the challenge of government.
In a letter he explained what he meant:
"It is not easy to subside," he wrote
To Mary Haddo, and again I quote,
"To the trend of common occupation."
Poor man, you can almost feel the frustration.

Aberdeen's successor

Who next? Well, anyone but Palmerston!
The Queen and Prince Albert, all said and done,
Loathed the man. Victoria had a list:
Derby... Lansdowne... Russell... You get the gist.
None was in a position to serve.
Clarendon refused, something of a nerve,
To support Derby, a condition
Made by 'Pam'. So, a coalition
Led by Derby hit the buffers. Lansdowne
Felt he was far too old, so turned it down.

Johnny Russell, that perennial clown,
Was delighted when the choice fell on him.
He must have been decidedly dim
To imagine, with the way he'd behaved,
That his colleagues would back him. So, depraved,
Vain and insufferable as he was,
The Queen sent for Lord Palmerston because,
Quite simply, he was the only man left.
Her Majesty, sad to say, was bereft.
She had even sounded out Clarendon,
Who declined. So 'Pumicestone' was the one.

Aberdeen, bless him, did his honest best
To urge his ex-colleagues, at his behest,
To support his old *bête noir*, Palmerston.
They rallied round and the battle was won...

Rhyming History

The course of the war

But not the war. The long campaign, sadly,
Was still going exceedingly badly.
The British public, of course, were gung-ho:
Pam was the man! It would soon be 'all go'!
A new Secretary of State for War,
A rotund old buffer called Lord Panmure,
Would put a bomb up the Ruskies, for sure!

It was change all round: poor old Menshikov
Was replaced by Prince Michael Gorchakov.
Nicholas had been mightily browned off
By Menshikov's woeful incompetence.
Gorchakov, able and full of good sense,
Offered a new lease of life to the Tsar.

Death of the Tsar

Or did he? It seems not. One step too far
Was Austria's professed intention
To join the allied coalition.
Nicholas, it appears, had had enough.
Tsars should perhaps be made of sterner stuff,
But in February he took to his bed,
With a severe chill. Within days he was dead.
The disasters of the campaign, it was said,
Had depressed his spirits and gone to his head.

The new Tsar, Alexander the Second,
Inherited, it's commonly reckoned,
An almost impossible legacy:
Industrial standstill, near bankruptcy,
Incompetence in the military...
And yet he declared (the height of folly)
That he would "perish rather than surrender".
He was the son of Tsar Nicholas, remember.

The Early Victorians

Stalemate

No surrender. Lord P was of like mind:
Alex and 'Pumicestone', two of a kind.
The PM feared Austria's involvement.
Extra support, fine, but not if this meant,
As he suspected, a premature peace.
The campaign needed some more elbow grease.
Lords Palmerston, Clarendon and Panmure
Blamed Raglan for the conduct of the war.

Poor Russell was packed off to Vienna
To talk peace, but I'd wager a tenner
That Britain's war aims would have to be met.
I am confident of winning my bet:
The new Prime Minister was on a roll,
Sebastopol his one and only goal.
As the Vienna talks entered stalemate,
The British Army was left to its fate.

Stalemate was also the name of the game
In the Crimea. It's a crying shame
That Canrobert was Commander-in-Chief
Of the French forces. It's my firm belief
That the Brits were fit and raring to go,
But was Canrobert ready? Sadly, no.

Raglan was a deeply frustrated man.
The allies lacked a comprehensive plan:
The British preferred an early assault;
The French demurred. This was Canrobert's fault.
His force was of superior strength, true.
The British were weak and this both men knew,
But little there was that Raglan could do
To redress the balance. Napoleon,
To the utter disgust of Palmerston,
Clarendon and most certainly Raglan,

Had forbidden Canrobert to attack –
Ordering him to hold his army back –
Unless he was sure that casualties
Would be light. It was orders such as these
That raised the question: how to defeat
The Russians when France was dragging her feet?

Following an artillery barrage
By the allies, Raglan felt, by and large,
That a combined assault was on the cards.
Canrobert offered his kindest regards,
But declined Raglan's invitation.
This was early April. Stagnation
Gave rise to furious frustration.

Raglan, a kindly man, was highly vexed.
Refusal to engage? Whatever next?
Even the pesky Russians were perplexed
By the allies' lack of will. Their fortress
Was open to attack. It was madness,
They felt, on the part of the enemy
Not to storm their vulnerable city.

Jean-Jacques Pélissier

Then a great change occurred. Oh, happy day!
Canrobert ('Robert-can't') resigned in May.
He had totally lost the plot, they say.
Succeeded by Jean-Jacques Pélissier,
Here at last was a chap who got things done.
Canrobert had been a figure of fun –
Not Pélissier! His manner was rough,
His tone direct and his discipline tough.
The French were a mess and he'd had enough.
Blessed with a fiery temper to boot,
He was bold, far-sighted and resolute.

A successful naval attack on Kertch
Left Sebastopol badly in the lurch.
On the Sea of Azov, this vital port
Was far from a stronghold of last resort.
It was central, rather, to the defence
Of the city. It made absolute sense
For the allies to starve Sebastopol
Of supplies. The fall of Kertch took its toll.
Essential lines of supply were breached.
A critical stage in the war was reached.

With Sebastopol weakened, Pélissier
Was increasingly sure he could win the day.
A French assault, at the very end of May,
On the Russian trenches, caused widespread dismay.
It cost 2,000 casualties – but hey,
This was hailed as a spectacular success.
Raglan felt some relief, he had to confess,
That events were finally moving forward.
The British had suffered nothing untoward,
While the damage the French caused was extensive.
The enemy was now on the defensive.

The allies prepared for a fresh offensive.
This was decided at a council of war
Between Raglan and Pélissier. The score,
Both were aware, in terms of casualties,
Would be great. But with the city on its knees,
A clear decision had to be taken.
Lord Raglan's resolve was sure and unshaken.

Attempted assault on Sebastopol

An attack was planned for the 7th of June.
For Raglan it came not a moment too soon.
The infantrymen, of course, would bear the brunt,
But the Brits presented a united front.

With the French they stormed the forward defences.
Would the Russians now come to their senses,
And raise the siege? Of course not. They took heart
From the fact that this was only a start.
The French had lost 5,000 men, the British
Some seven hundred. They'd fight to the finish.

The allies, however, were far from put off.
The French were focused on the 'Malakov',
So-called, a major fortification
Within Sebastopol, but a station
Bristling with Russian artillery.
Some considered such an attack plain silly,
But Pélissier was determined. Raglan,
For his part, set his sights on the 'Great Redan',
To the south of the Malakov. Thus began,
On the 17th of June, the next assault.
The outcome was utter disaster. Whose fault?

Pélissier's, mainly, no shadow of doubt.
Obsessed, some felt, with the Malakov 'redoubt',
He attacked far too early in the morning.
At 3, even before the day was dawning,
And without giving Raglan enough warning,
He gave the command for the French to advance.
Why? His men didn't stand the ghost of a chance.
Moreover, there was not a cloud in the sky,
So when Raglan (with no choice but to comply)
Mustered his men in support of his ally,
The Russians were ready. First the French fell,
Overwhelmed by a hail of bullets, pell-mell.
Poor Raglan, horrified, knew only too well
That he had to engage and join the attack.
To be seen to hesitate now, to hold back,
And to leave the valiant French to their fate,
Was a shame too terrible to contemplate.

So, Heaven help them, the British infantry,
Facing the full force of the artillery,
Charged towards the Russian guns – a hail storm.
Every man had his duty to perform,
"In the teeth," as they said, "of a living gale".
The hazardous attack was destined to fail.
Pélissier, at least, accepted the blame,
The assault forever a blot on his name.
Casualties? Once more, a hideous cost:
On the French side, 3,500 lost;
On the British, just under half that figure.
Yet the allied siege continued with vigour.

The death of Raglan

Raglan was in a sad state, a broken man.
The disastrous assault on the Great Redan
Was a cruel blow and proved the final straw.
Roebuck's report on the conduct of the war,

Rhyming History

Published only a matter of days before,
Laid a fair measure of blame at Raglan's door.
Coupled with constant carping from Lord Panmure,
The Commander-in-Chief was finished, for sure.

Within nine days of the Great Redan attack,
Tired and sick at heart, he was on the rack.
Struck down with diarrhoea, he took to his bed.
There was no hope. Two days later he was dead.

History has been less than kind to Raglan.
A mild man, he was no Duke of Wellington,
But he earned the trust and respect of his men.
He scored, as a strategist, six out of ten –
Not enough, I hear you cry, and you'd be right.
Blessed with no particular flair or foresight,
He nonetheless kept the flame of hope alive
Among his troops. Canrobert lacked dash and drive,
But Raglan proved a dependable ally.
His code of honour was strong: "to do and die",
In Tennyson's immortal words. That is why,
However hard the commentators may try,
I stand by Raglan. He was dealt a bad hand.
Old-fashioned, yes, that I can understand –
But unaccommodating or divisive?
Never. At times he could be indecisive.
That was a fault. But Raglan led from the front.
He won the favour of his men. To be blunt,
The feeble politicians were to blame.

It is with an overwhelming sense of shame
That folk today remember his Lordship's name.
For Raglan was made a scapegoat. No statue
Was raised in his honour. This is sadly true.
Florence Nightingale, who was hardly a fan,
Left these well-chosen words in praise of Raglan:
No great general, "but a very good man".

Raglan's successor

The non-entity who succeeded him
Was Major-General James Simpson. Dim,
Incompetent and unambitious,
Panmure should have become suspicious
When Simpson told him he found it "irksome"
To have to deal with allies! The outcome,
Of course, was unhappy. Pélissier
Took responsibility, day to day,
For the conduct of the allied campaign.
The British came under increasing strain,
As Simpson's faults were harder to ignore.
The ex-Secretary of State for War,
Lord Newcastle, came out on a visit.
He thought Simpson the absolute limit:
"A raving lunatic" – his very words.

The thought of winning was now for the birds.
All was muddle! All was confusion!
To bring the war to a conclusion,
What, in God's name, were the British to do?
With Simpson in command, nobody knew.

A fresh Russian attack

The Russians had little hope of success.
How long they could hold out was anyone's guess,
But the writing was finally on the wall.
Their defences were not bearing up at all.
The city was far from a bottomless pit,
And Gorchakov was all too aware of it.
He warned Alexander. His words cut no ice.
The Tsar was adamant. Peace at any price
Was anathema. So, however absurd,
A strategy was hatched in St. Petersburg

To launch an offensive. This hardly made sense.
There is a saying: the best form of defence
Is attack. This proved to be fatally wrong.

Gorchakov made it up as he went along.
On the 16th of August he made his move.
The allies (touching wood) could only approve:
They had forewarning. The plan had been discussed
In Berlin, to Tsar Alexander's disgust.
Indeed, it had been reported in the press!
Even Simpson was ready (well, more or less)
And Pélissier was primed and well prepared.

Few, it seems, among the Russians were spared:
4,000 wounded, over 2,000 dead,
And thousands missing. How Sebastopol bled.
Allied casualties, it has to be said,
Were not insignificant: 2,000 killed,
Or wounded. Napoleon was far from thrilled.
He bombarded the hapless Pélissier
With hysterical demands that, come what may,
Casualties be kept to a minimum.
Easily said, and all very well for some,
But to sit around in Paris on his bum,
While his army were blasted to kingdom come…
Napoleon should have kept well out of it –
Our friend Pélissier had no doubt of it.

However, with the Russians on the run,
Pélissier's orders from Napoleon
Were to press his advantage. All said and done,
The Emperor changed his tune from day to day.
The allies resolved, without further delay,
To force the issue to a conclusion.
In a state of terminal confusion,
The enemy could do little but panic.
Gorchakov, however (and this was tragic),

Was still receiving strict orders from the Tsar
To stand firm – ridiculous, but there you are.
The poor fellow was too weak to disobey,
And up to 2,000 Russians a day
Met their end during the final bombardment.
Death, the ultimate recruiting sergeant,
Enjoyed a field day as Sebastopol fell.

The fall of Sebastopol

The Malakov was taken. The French did well –
The British less so. Two hundred yards of ground
Lay between them and the Great Redoubt. They found,
To their bewilderment and utter horror,
That they came under heavy fire. Honour,
The only currency of any value
In time of war, was, I regret to tell you,
Among the British in short supply that day.
Several soldiers simply ran away;
Others held their ground, but refused to go in.
They disobeyed orders, the ultimate sin.

Gorchakov was forced to withdraw nonetheless.
The assault was deemed an overall success,
As Pélissier drove the enemy out.
The result, however, was far from a rout.
The allies failed to pursue the enemy:
The shattered remnants of the Russian army
Blew up ammunition stores in their wake,
Sank their remaining ships and, for safety's sake,
Exploded the bridge over which they had crossed,
To the north of the city. All was not lost.

It was left to the allies to count the cost:
Some 13,000 Russian casualties;
10,000 French and British – and this, if you please,
Was hailed by *all* as the mother of victories.

Rhyming History

Mary Seacole's contribution

Talking of mothers, it was Mary Seacole,
The first woman to enter Sebastopol
After the city fell to the allies,
Who noted, having seen with her own eyes,
What she described as "that harrowing sight" –
A most terrible spectacle, the plight
Of thousands of Russians left behind
At that "woeful hospital". Few were blind
To their suffering, the poor men dying
In their hundreds, in agony, crying,
Begging for release from their dreadful fate.

The wounded were in a pitiful state,
"Without assistance". The doctors had fled –
Cowardice writ large, it has to be said.

Mother Seacole discovered some brown bread,
Still in the oven, at the Great Redan.
A series of adventures now began
For this strange old woman. A complex soul,
She took to looting in Sebastopol:
A cracked china teapot, a parasol
And a bell that she bore away proudly
"On my saddle". She even bragged loudly
Of a "decorated altar candle"
That she presented (too hot to handle? –
A smart move) to the Commander-in-Chief!

She did not consider herself a thief,
But the risk she took was beyond belief.
From "a little French soldier" she bought
An altar picture (she was never caught) –
This of the Madonna. She brought it home.
Well, you know what they say: "When in Rome…"

The Early Victorians

Mary's progress was slightly alarming.
"My restaurant was always full" – charming,
Surrounded as she was by the starving,
Dying and wounded in equal measure,
Surely no occasion for pleasure.

Foreign trippers arrived for their leisure,
Enjoying picnics, taking photographs,
Sketching the ruins and looking for laughs.

There was hunting (strictly for the hearties);
There were cricket matches, dinner parties,
Even amateur theatricals – yes,
It pains me deeply, I have to confess,
But Mother Seacole found time to obsess
With costumes, with wigs and with fancy dress,
In the midst of all this pain and distress.

She did ask one important question:
"What was to be done?" The suggestion

Of a siege of the north, of more fighting
And of more bloodshed was uninviting.

Mary herself failed to offer a view.
That was for the powers-that-be to do,
"The business," in her words, "of a few
"At headquarters" (this was certainly true)
"And in council at home". Nobody knew,
In truth, how to bring this terrible war
To an end, or what it had all been for.

The next move

So, what to do next? Answer came there none.
So much, and yet so little, had been done.
If you cared to listen to Palmerston,
The Crimean conflict was far from won.
He would grind the Tsar's nose into the dust –
Three years it could take, he wasn't that fussed.
Peace feelers were not on the agenda!

Austria was still the main offender
With respect to seeking a compromise.
Russia, too (an unwelcome surprise),
Was bent on continuing the campaign.

The French, however, had little to gain
From fighting on. Their troops were on a high,
Their honour satisfied. So why, oh why,
Did Napoleon bow to Palmerston
In his dogged resolve to carry on?

The war was now unpopular in France.
Pélissier felt they should take a chance
And sue for peace. He strongly resisted
His boss, but Napoleon insisted.

The Early Victorians

Pélissier's men suffered terribly
That second winter. It was sad to see.
From the first few days of January
To the end of March 1856,   **1856**
Cholera and typhus, a deadly mix,
Swept through the ranks of the French. Few were spared.
30,000 perished. Nobody cared.
Napoleon's fault? No one would have dared
Blame the Emperor, but I have to say,
Had he stopped to listen to Pélissier,
Many would have lived to fight another day.

The British troops weathered the winter well.
They suffered, as we saw, a living hell
The year before. Now they were well supplied
With warm clothes and were more than satisfied:
Boots, mufflers and woollies on the outside,
And hot, nourishing food on the inside!
It did not take the Brits long to decide
To share their good fortune with their allies,
The French: medicines and other supplies,
Chocolate and treats, a welcome surprise.

Simpson had continued to be clueless,
Weak and incompetent, worse than useless.
Charged by Panmure with utter idleness,
With creating, in short, a fine old mess,
He resigned in the autumn. No great loss,
And soon forgotten, what of his boss,
Lord Panmure himself? It does make me cross
That Simpson was made to shoulder the blame.
For where was his Lordship, in Heaven's name,
Or old 'Pumicestone' himself, come to that?
In another world, or I'll eat my hat.
Inflict defeat on the Russians? How?
Bring on the peace and bring it on now!

Rhyming History

The Paris Congress

The Prime Minister was forced to give in.
This was clearly a war no one could win.
The French had been putting out peace feelers,
It emerged (classic wheelers and dealers),
Ever since entering Sebastopol.
The war had taken a terrible toll,
But Palmerston still refused to be rushed.
The Tsar was a threat. He had to be crushed.
The silly old buffer was overruled
By his own Cabinet. Pam, don't be fooled,
Was highly aggrieved their ardour had cooled.

There were talks about talks, then still more talks.
The doves, thank the Lord, outnumbered the hawks.
Palmerston, to cut a long story short,
After hoping the talks would come to nought,
Agreed to the so-called 'Paris Congress'.
In spite of Clarendon's flair and *finesse*,
Britain was outmanoeuvred. Have no doubt,
The deal that was finally hammered out
Had something in it for everyone.
Well, that is the essence, all said and done,
Of any effective peace agreement.

The treaty, though, was a mixed achievement,
Given the horrific cost of the war.
Britain was pushing at an open door,
But in the event won few concessions.
Russia kept most of her possessions,
But was forced to give up Bessarabia,
On the lower Danube, to Moldavia.
Along with her close neighbour, Wallachia,
Both were guaranteed their independence.
The Treaty of Paris made the most sense

The Early Victorians

When it came to the case of the Black Sea,
Its waters closed in perpetuity
To all warships. The sea was neutralised,
In effect. The Russians were surprised
That fortresses were also forbidden.
They balked at this, but were overridden.
This was designed to stop Russia, plainly,
Ever again intimidating Turkey.
Dream on! As early as 1870,
The Russians began to refortify.
Nobody stopped them. They didn't even try.

Back to Paris. One particular success
Was that henceforth there would be open access
To the Danube for ships of all nations.
The Sultan joined in the celebrations,
Having chalked up one strong gain in Turkey's name:
The Tsar of Russia relinquished all claim
Over the Sultan's Christian subjects
In the Ottoman. One of the defects,
Hand on heart, of the Treaty of Paris,
And one that it's all too easy to miss,
Is that there were very few guarantees
For its enforcement. Clauses such as these
Could be signed up to, then broken with ease.

So it was with this undertaking too.
There was little that the allies could do,
When Russia, in 1876,
Tore up her promises. Up to her old tricks,
In a seedy display of histrionics,
She assumed the role of 'protector' of Slavs
And Christians both. She did nothing by halves.

This was disappointing. Be that as it may,
That's another story for another day.

The Crimean War was over. Good riddance.
Little was achieved and even less made sense.
Lord Palmerston professed himself delighted
With the Paris peace. Don't get too excited.
His Lordship could believe what he wanted to,
Corrupt and disingenuous through and through.

The Victoria Cross

For Britain's victory the Queen gave thanks.
A cross of merit, open to all ranks,
She inaugurated 'for bravery'.
Some deemed it little short of knavery
To single out 'the brave'. What a disgrace!
Bravery and courage were commonplace,
A solemn duty, on the battlefield.

The Queen was sensible enough to yield:
The Victoria Cross bore the legend
'For Valour'. Nobody could now pretend
That this failed to mark the true heroes out –
The highest accolade, without a doubt,
For acts of conspicuous gallantry.
There's no greater honour than the VC.

The Early Victorians

In Hyde Park, before an enormous crowd **1857**
Of 100,000 cheering aloud,
Victoria, in full dress uniform,
And on horseback, took the people by storm.

Sixty-two crosses she presented that day,
A true measure of the courage on display –
These the veterans of the Crimean War.
Indeed, we are told, there were some fifty more
Still to be awarded. That day in late June,
1857, that fine afternoon,
The time had arrived, not a moment too soon,
To honour the heroes of the Crimea.

The medal had been Prince Albert's idea.
Was he given credit for this? No fear!
The Queen could do no wrong. Albert, alas,
Was too German. This was not only crass,
But a mockery, given that 'Victoire',
The Queen's outspoken and tactless 'mama',
Was pure German. On her late father's side,
You would have to go back (just a rough guide)
Down six or seven generations,
Through scores of Teutonic relations,
Before a non-German prince or princess
Entered the gene pool. I couldn't care less.
Her background matters not a jot to me,
But it's tantamount to hypocrisy
That Albert was given such a rough ride.

Too German by half? Well, you can decide,
But to my mind his elevation
To Prince Consort gave him a station
Commensurate with his talents. The Queen
Was delighted. Far too long it had been
Since she had first sought recognition
Of Albert's worth. His new position

Was announced to the world the selfsame day –
A happy accident, I'm pleased to say –
That Victoria honoured those heroes
Of the Crimea. The first that she chose,
For outstanding valour three years before,
Was Ship's Mate Charles Lucas. During the war
He picked up a shell with a burning fuse
Aboard HMS Hecla. Not good news,
A live explosive. He earned his award
For calmly lobbing the shell overboard,
Saving the lives of the entire crew.

The recipients are a select few.
For leading five of his colleagues to safety
In Iraq, Lance Sergeant Johnson Beharry,
A true hero of our time, won the VC.
Queen Elizabeth's words, chosen carefully,
Were apt. "It's been rather a long time," she said,
"Since I've awarded one of these." A cool head,
Had Beharry. One can only admire
His breathtaking gallantry under fire.

The Indian Mutiny

As folk were enjoying their holiday
In Hyde Park, some four thousand miles away,
In India, trouble was breaking out
North-east of Delhi. There is little doubt
That the Indian Mutiny, so-called,
Had complex roots. Landowners stood appalled
As inheritance laws were overhauled,
Depriving them of their property rights.
This was one of many 'reforming' kites
Flown by the East India Company,
Or at least on its behalf. Subtly,
Slowly, the Brits were tightening their grip –
In economics, trade, land ownership

The Early Victorians

And religion. Take the missionary,
Spreading the word of Christianity
Throughout the Indian sub-continent –
A source of misgiving and discontent.

But it was in the Indian army
That dissent spread. In the military,
The British were in a minority
Of one in seven (a rough estimate).
Up in Bengal (again, approximate),
Of 150,000 troops,
Just 20,000 were British. No dupes,
The Indian officers (or 'sepoys')
Were key. You could tell the men from the boys,
Honour, loyalty and trust their proud claim.

So whatever occurred, in Heaven's name,
To explain the truly shameful events
Of the 9th of May? They barely made sense.
It was an overcast, oppressive day –
An ominous sign, I regret to say.
At Meermut, on the army parade ground,
Eighty-five sepoy troops, with their hands bound,
Were stripped of their uniforms. There and then,
Their legs and arms were manacled. Proud men,
Who boasted years of glorious service,
What on earth had they done to deserve this?

The cause of the unrest

The Enfield rifle, oddly, was the cause.
Most British officers were dinosaurs
And merited little or no applause
For their unprecedented lack of tact
In overlooking one distasteful fact.
The rumours had been flying thick and fast
That the cartridges (sepoys were aghast)

Were greased with forbidden animal fat,
Pork or beef – as unsavoury as that.
Muslims and Hindus were less than enthralled:
The cartridges, before being installed,
Needed their paper ends removed, with teeth,
To expose the powder. It's my belief
That this led directly to mutiny.

It is now reckoned highly unlikely
That the cartridges sent out to Delhi
And its neighbouring regions were greased
With fat from any prohibited beast.
But the facts were widely ignored, of course,
As the rumour mongers came out in force.
Refusal to handle the cartridges
Led to withdrawal of privileges –

The Early Victorians

Nay, the shackling and imprisonment
Of the Meermut sepoys. As discontent
Spread, like wild fire, the chaos began.
The aggrieved sepoys rose up to a man
To release their comrades. Like it or not,
When the first British officer was shot,
It was more than likely that the culprit
Was a sepoy. The tragic truth of it
Is that wiser heads had seen this coming.

The bloodshed, sickening and mind-numbing,
Was triggered by 'conduct unbecoming' –
The ugly, humiliating treatment
Of the sepoys. The Brits, to this extent,
Were responsible. There was no excuse,
Nonetheless, for the hideous abuse
Suffered at the hands of the common mob.
Looting, burning, they did a thorough job –
Murder and mayhem. Dozens lost their lives,
Including children. The record survives.

Terrible atrocities

There was worse to come. The marauding hordes
Set off for Delhi, to seek fresh rewards.
Three native regiments were stationed there.
The British officers were in despair:
They lacked support and their numbers were few.
They put up a fight, but what could they do?
Whole families were massacred – women,
Butchered as they fled, defenceless children
And babes in arms. Outrages such as these,
The Meermut and Delhi atrocities,
Gave rise to desperate acts of vengeance
On a hideous scale. Guilt? Innocence?
Who cared? To the Brits it made little sense

Rhyming History

To discriminate between right and wrong.
They made the rules up as they went along.
This we shall see, but sadly not before
We visit the old stronghold of Kanpur.
For here was the worst example, for sure,
Of the savagery – nay, treachery –
Unleashed by the terrible mutiny.

The outrage at Kanpur

Kanpur was a key strategic city.
The British garrison, more's the pity,
Was manned by sixty artillerymen.
They were greatly outnumbered yet again,
As Kanpur soldiers made up the rest.
Sepoys against the British: no contest.
Should the native Indians mutiny,
General Sir Hugh Wheeler's first duty
Would be to save the women and children.

The storm, when it came, was swift and sudden,
But Nana Sahib, a local princeling,
Volunteered to do a wonderful thing.
Proposing a compromise to Wheeler,
He put out the following peace feeler:
In exchange for the latter's surrender –
The British were on the ropes, remember –
He offered safe passage down the Ganges
For the dozens of British families
Facing almost certain death in Kanpur.
Three hundred women and children, or more,
Took to the boats, all with awnings of straw –
"Rather like floating haystacks," someone said.

Sir Hugh had been seriously misled
By Nana Sahib. No sooner afloat,
Arrows were shot onto every boat –

Flaming torches. The Brits opened fire.
The convoy, like a funeral pyre,
Floated on, amazingly, for two days.

The poor wretched souls who survived the blaze
Were set upon as soon as they landed.
The men had been killed, their wives left stranded,
Their little ones bereft. Without mercy,
The assassins rounded them up. Thirsty,
Hungry, exhausted, their nerves shot to bits,
There was worse to come. Scared out of their wits,
They were dragged to a place called 'Bibighur' –
Or the 'House of Ladies', if you prefer
(Some irony) – where they were put to death.

Forgive me, perhaps I should save my breath,
But the truth must be told. Into a well
They were thrown, a veritable hell,
For some of the victims were still alive.
It would be impossible to contrive

Rhyming History

An end more gruesome, a more cruel fate.
That deadly and desperate potentate,
The Nana, was to blame, no doubt of it.
He tried, of course, to wriggle out of it.

Horrible acts of vengeance

The news was met with stupefaction
When word reached London. The reaction,
However, on the ground to these outrages
Was worse than grotesque. I could cover pages
Detailing the obscene acts of vengeance
That followed. The British made little pretence
At justice, mercy (God forbid!) or fair play,
Unbridled revenge the order of the day.
India had sinned, so India must pay.

There is evidence that at the Bibighur
Sepoys refused to take part in the murder.
Five local butchers were left to massacre
The innocent victims. Yet orders went out
To punish the sepoys. Policy throughout
Was to degrade these men and to break their caste.
Beef and pork were stuffed down their throats. I'm aghast.
Prisoners had to lick the blood off the floor
Of the infamous Bibighur. At Kanpur
Old men and their grandchildren were burnt alive.

The thirst for revenge went into overdrive,
As Brigadier John Nicholson, at Delhi –
No namby-pamby, no yellow-belly he –
Proposed flaying alive the perpetrators
Of the late horrors, be they agitators
Or mere lookers-on. To account for their sins,
Devout Muslims were sewn into pig skins
And, prior to being hanged, smeared with pork fat.
I ask you, how vile and hideous is that?

The Early Victorians

Hanging parties of volunteers were arranged
To round up victims. The British were deranged.
William Russell, of *The Times*, bore witness
To one prisoner, to force him to confess,
Roasted, in agony, on an open spit –
Oh, the terror and the cruelty of it.
Another 'sport' was to strap an Indian,
Picked at random, to the mouth of a cannon,
To be blown to smithereens by grapeshot –
This for pure entertainment, like it or not.

What was the Prime Minister doing the while?
With the smiling cunning of a crocodile,
Old Palmerston kept his cards close to his chest.
The British, he reckoned, were doing their best
To suppress the mutiny. He was cheerful
And relaxed. Where Victoria was tearful
(And angry), his complacency was fearful.
The Queen denounced him for his incompetence.

'Clemency' Canning

Worse still, the PM said little in defence
Of Lord Canning, the Governor-General.
Palmerston must have known only too well
That the Governor faced a huge dilemma.
A sympathetic, level-headed fella,
Canning was well aware of the crying need
To punish the recreants. But he paid heed
To the equally pressing necessity
For justice, fair play and sensitivity.
India was a powder keg. A cool head
Was critical. The mutiny never spread
Beyond the central northern sector. Lahore,
In the Punjab, was unaffected. Mysore,
Calcutta, Hyderabad and Bangalore
Were untouched and managed to uphold the law.

Rhyming History

Canning should take much of the credit for this.
His role was key, but would be easy to miss,
Given his drubbing at the hands of the press.
Reproached as a milksop by *The Times*, no less,
'Clemency Canning' they dubbed him. How profound!

They called for Delhi to be razed to the ground,
For all Muslim mosques to be torched. A disgrace.
For a sepoy there was no more fitting place
Than a gable-end or the branch of a tree –
To hang there, you understand. Take it from me,
Any such gruesome, benighted policy
Would have fuelled the flames of the Mutiny.

Yet in the midst of this, 'Mr. Clemency',
So-called, poor Canning, had the temerity
To issue orders to the British Army
To execute those who had committed crimes,
But those only. This occasioned *The Times*
To proclaim his Lordship some kind of nutter –
Viz. "a prim philanthropist from Calcutta".

Weighing in, the Army's Commander-in-Chief,
The Duke of Cambridge, almost beyond belief,
Was hopeful "that no undue leniency
"Will be adopted". He was sure "the country
"Will support all those who have the manliness
"To inflict the punishment". A fine old mess.
Without Lord Canning's insistence on fairness,
Justice (however rough) and the rule of law,
There would have been serious trouble in store.

The Prime Minister took an age to come round.
Canning's Indian policy was unsound,
Untimely and dangerous. Clemency? Pah!
He would annul the order! One step too far,

The Early Victorians

Cried the Cabinet. So Palmerston gave way.
His support of Canning, I am bound to say,
Was begrudging. However, come what may,
Even *The Times*, baying for blood remember,
Changed its tune when finally, in September,
Delhi fell to the British. Sad to relate,
The revolt dragged on. Only in '58   **1858**
Was Lucknow, three months under siege, retaken.

The good Queen, unless I am much mistaken,
Supported Canning's spirit of forgiveness.
There was "indiscriminate vindictiveness"
Among the English community abroad,
Reported Canning, and he was not ignored.
Rancour and revenge Victoria deplored.
She shared the "sorrow and indignation"
Evinced by Canning. The British nation
Had shown, in its discrimination
Against sepoys, an "unchristian spirit".

Lord Palmerston was the absolute limit,
But this was one battle he would never win.
"There is no hatred," she wrote, "of a brown skin."
The Queen meant it. The reality, of course,
Was different. The British, without remorse,
Conducted themselves with a savagery
Unprecedented in our long history.
How peace was restored is a strange mystery.
Most Indians remained respectful and true,
Mutiny and murder the work of the few.

One major political casualty
Was the age-old East India Company.
The British government took over control
Of India. The Empire was on a roll.
Canning reaped his reward, becoming Viceroy.
So Palmerston got his comeuppance. What joy!

Palmerston resigns

Happily, by the time he was appointed,
Palmerston had lost office. Disappointed,
And not a little angry, Pam was tripped up
By Disraeli, no less, the arrogant pup,
Over the Conspiracy to Murder Bill.
Defeated in the Commons (a bitter pill),
Pam resigned three days later. For good or ill,
He had introduced hasty legislation
After the attempted assassination
Of the French Emperor, Napoleon the Third.

Although unlikely, and not a little absurd,
It appeared (as details of the plot unravelled)
That Felice Orsini (the suspect) had travelled,
On a British passport, with bombs that had been made
In Birmingham. Palmerston was duly dismayed.
The Bill he proposed would make it a felony,
Carrying with it the heaviest penalty,
To plot in England to kill a person abroad.

This was a measure the country could ill afford,
According to the radicals. Oddly enough,
The Tories, who should have been made of sterner stuff,
Agreed, and Palmerston was soundly defeated –
By nineteen votes. Pam, we're told, had become heated
And shaken his fist at the opposition.
He was accused (a man in his position!)
Of kowtowing to Emperor Napoleon.
The Tories seized their chance. Curtains for Palmerston.

Re-enter Derby

Lord Derby's second administration,
Of fifteen and a half months' duration,

Achieved little. The new ministry saw through
The Government of India Act. All knew,
Of course, that old Pam had begun the process
And would have boasted a personal success
Had he not been obliged to settle for less –
A spell in the political wilderness.
So Derby took full credit for the reform.

Minority government, never the norm,
Was the unlucky Earl's undignified lot:
Three stints in just sixteen years, I kid you not.

This second time round brought little that was new,
Unless, that is, you happened to be a Jew.
The Jews Relief Act, sadly long overdue,
Gave Jews the right to sit in Parliament,
Ending years of injustice and discontent.

Rhyming History

The Queen's young family

Queen Victoria had nine pregnancies
In seventeen years. She hated babies!
She said they looked like frogs, and resented
The challenge that they clearly presented
To her comfortable family life –
By which I mean her pleasures as a wife.
All her nine children survived infancy,
And all lived to marry, as we shall see.

Marriage of the Princess Royal

The Princess Royal, known as Vicky,
The eldest child of Albert and the Queen,
Became engaged, at the age of fourteen,
To Prince Frederick of Prussia. This,
Sadly, gave rise to bitter prejudice
In Germany, where the 'English Princess',
As she was dubbed (she was briefly Empress),
Was unpopular for no good reason.
Xenophobia, ever in season,
Is a poison – nationalism, too.

Prince Frederick (or 'Fritz') was, in my view,
A liberal, broad-minded sort of chap.
He suffered the unfortunate mishap
Of dying after just ninety-nine days
As Emperor. Fritz was beyond all praise.
He shared the thoughts of his father-in-law,
Prince Albert. His utter hatred of war
Held true promise for the new Germany.

It was sadly a different journey
Following his premature death. His son –
Kaiser Wilhelm the Second, that's the one –

The Early Victorians

Had other ideas. The First World War
Was the upshot. That's for later, for sure,
But 1914 was not far away.

When Princess Vicky, on her wedding day,
In 1858, married her Fritz,
The Queen and Albert were tickled to bits.
Though the Prince would miss his favourite child,
Frederick was a catch. The crowds went wild.
Vicky was beautiful, bright and serene,
A Prussian Princess at seventeen.
The royal family was riding high.

The crowning irony, hard to deny,
Is that Queen Victoria's first grandson,
The troublesome Kaiser, all said and done,
Adored his grandma. The damage he did
She never lived to see. Heaven forbid.

Bibliography

David Cecil, *Melbourne* (Constable, 1965)

Roger Ellis, *Who's Who in Victorian Britain* (Shepheard-Walwyn, 1997)

Norman Gash, *Peel* (Longman, 1976)

Christopher Harvie, *Revolution and the Rule of Law (1789-1851)* (in *The Oxford History of Britain,* ed. Kenneth O. Morgan – Oxford University Press, 2001)

Richard Holmes, *Wellington, The Iron Duke* (Harper Collins, 2003)

Walter E. Houghton, *The Victorian Frame of Mind, 1830-1870* (Yale University Press, 1957)

Douglas Hurd, *Robert Peel, A Biography* (Phoenix, 2008)

Lucille Iremonger, *Lord Aberdeen* (Collins, 1978)

Dorothy Marshall, *The Life and Times of Victoria* (Weidenfeld & Nicolson, with Book Club Associates, 1972)

H. C. G. Matthew, *The Liberal Age (1852-1914)* (in *The Oxford History of Britain,* ed. Kenneth O. Morgan – Oxford University Press, 2001)

Michael Patterson, *A Brief History of Life in Victorian Britain* (Constable & Robinson, 2008)

John Prest, *Lord John Russell* (Macmillan, 1972)

Stuart J. Reid, *Lord John Russell* (Sampson Low, Marston and Company, 1895)

K. D. Reynolds and H. C. G. Matthew, *Queen Victoria* (Oxford University Press, 2007)

Jasper Ridley, *Lord Palmerston* (Panther Books, 1972)

Trevor Royle, *Crimea – The Great Crimean War, 1854-1856* (Abacus, 2000)

Mary Seacole, *Wonderful Adventures of Mrs. Mary Seacole in Many Lands* (ed. Sara Salih) (Penguin, 2005)

Michael Slater, *Charles Dickens* (Oxford University Press, 2007)

Donald Southgate, *The Most English Minister – The Policies and Politics of Palmerston* (Macmillan, 1966)

G. M. Trevelyan, *A Shortened History of England* (Penguin, 1959)

A. N. Wilson, *The Victorians* (Hutchinson, 2002)

A. N. Wilson, *Victoria, A Life* (Atlantic Books, 2015)

RHYMING HISTORY
The Story of England in Verse

EARLIER VOLUMES IN THE SERIES

Volume One: 55BC – 1485
THE ROMANS TO THE WARS OF THE ROSES

An entertaining, ironic and accessible journey through our history from the first arrival of Julius Caesar in 55BC to the defeat of Richard the Third at Bosworth Field in 1485.

An ebook of Volume One and a CD of excerpts are also available.

Volume Two: 1485 – 1603
THE TUDORS

From Henry the Seventh to Queen Elizabeth, this volume spans one of the most exciting, turbulent and colourful periods of English history.

Volume Three: 1603 – 1649
THE EARLY STUARTS AND CIVIL WAR

Where James the First was intelligent and astute, his son was obstinate and rash. Charles the First plunged his kingdom into bloody civil war.

Volume Four: 1649 – 1660
CROMWELL AND THE COMMONWEALTH

This volume charts the early success and final decline of
the Commonwealth, closing with the triumphant return of
Charles the Second to reclaim his lost kingdom.

Volume Five: 1660 – 1685
CHARLES THE SECOND AND THE RESTORATION

The Restoration of Charles the Second ushered in a new
age of scandal, danger and political turmoil. The cast of
characters is rich and diverse.

Volume Six: 1685 – 1688
JAMES THE SECOND, THE FORGOTTEN KING

James the Second was headstrong and inept. He inherited a kingdom at peace, but rebellion was in the air. The Glorious Revolution was about to begin.

Volume Seven: 1688 – 1714
GLORIOUS REVOLUTION,
THE LAST OF THE STUARTS

In the Glorious Revolution, King William and Queen Mary were invited to reign jointly. When Queen Anne died childless, the Stuart dynasty drew to a close.

Volume Eight: 1714 – 1760
THE EARLY HANOVERIANS

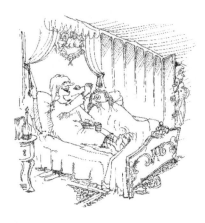

The accession of George the First ushered in an era of change. The turbulent reign of George the Second ended with the celebrated Year of Victories.

Volume Nine: 1760 – 1789
GEORGE THE THIRD AND THE LOSS OF AMERICA

The reign of 'Farmer George' was the third longest in British history, but the first signs of the King's madness were beginning to show.

Volume Ten: 1789 - 1837
THE LAST OF THE HANOVERIANS

These were momentous times: the rise of Napoleon, the Great Reform Act and the abolition of the slave trade. With the death of William the Fourth the Hanoverian era was at an end.

TO BE PUBLISHED IN 2021

Volume Twelve: 1858 – 1901
THE LATER VICTORIANS

With the death of Queen Victoria, Great Britain faced an uncertain future. An amazing age of invention and political progress had drawn to a close.

Please visit our website for excerpts from all these volumes and for news of performances of the verse.

www.rhyminghistory.co.uk

Printed in Great Britain
by Amazon